# The Questions
*Classic Edition*

By the same authors


**The Questions – Retro Edition**
*ISBN 1-904999-10-7*

**The Questions - First Compendium Edition**
*ISBN 1-904999-11-5*

# The Questions
## Classic Edition

Fiona McCade

William O'Leary

Cath Sutton

Kennedy & Boyd

Published by
Kennedy and Boyd
an imprint of
Zeticula
57 St Vincent Crescent
Glasgow
G3 8NQ

http://www.kennedyandboyd.co.uk
admin@kennedyandboyd.co.uk

First published in 2004




## ISBN 1-904999-09-3 Paperback



http://www.thequestions.co.uk

# Acknowledgements

Cath, Fiona and William would like to thank all these lovely people for their invaluable help, their forthright opinions and their unfailing commitment to trivia: Libby Bell, Marcus Berkmann, Matthew Brander, Donald Brown, James Costain, A.J Cotter, Dylan Dowd, Petula Dowe, Ceri Essex, Jes Fernie, Kirsty Fulford, John Gore, Mike Griffiths, Iain Harper, Stuart Johnston, Jennifer Jones, Peter Jones, Paul Kent, Andrew Leith, James Leslie, John Macgill, Chris Maguire, Ian Marr, James McCade, Shirley McCade, Roy McMillan, Patricia 'Dandelion and Burdock' Miller, Robert and Helen Miller, Heather Montgomery, Richard Phillips, Maria Quinn, Anna Redfern, Elisabeth Reissner, Jeanne Saint, Jude Sim, George Sutton, Vivian Sutton, Wal Sutton, Janet de Vigne, Abigail Youngman.

# Introduction

Have you ever fallen madly in love, only to discover that the object of your affections has a jar-a-day Marmite habit and from that moment, you know you have to leave? Possibly not, but there remains the terrifying possibility that something so apparently trivial could bring an entire relationship to its knees.

The little things in life can often cause the biggest explosions in the minefield of compatibility. What hope is there for any union if she wants diamonds, but he keeps giving her pearls? Or if you prefer the back row, but your prospective mate insists on sitting at the front? You might think all is lost, but never fear, the Questions are here. They are the simplest, most effective way of cutting right to the core of the compatibility dilemma and the fastest, cheapest route to finding your perfect partner, whether in love, business, friendship or bridge.

The Questions deal with the most crucial aspects of everyday existence, like popcorn, TV and superheroes. Religion, politics, ethics and genetics are hard to ignore, but we've tried. After all, are they really so important? Are they honestly more vital to happiness than a firm consensus on whether Starsky is better than Hutch?

Ask somebody - anybody - a Question and you're guaranteed an instant, yet profound, insight into their psyche. Take this book to a first meeting and you'll know within seconds if it's worth taking your coat off.

The rules are simple. Each Question offers an either/or choice. All you need to find out is which of the two alternatives your subject prefers. That's it. Only one, straightforward response is required. Tell people who say "What if..?" and "How can I reply to that unless..?" to shut up and answer. It's not necessary to know anything to have an opinion. Ask any politician.

Most importantly, once they have answered, they must explain their reasons. This is the most interesting bit, because it reveals how their minds work and what they are really like. To get you into the mood for discussion, we've shared our own, humble opinions on each Question. Obviously, no Question has a definitive answer. The right reply is the one you like best.

Even if your prospective partner finds it impossible to give you a straight answer, you are still getting priceless information regarding their ability to make other life choices. Remember, the people who can't answer the Questions are the very ones who will shout "I don't know! I don't know!" when you ask them which exit to take at the next roundabout. You might think you've found the girl of your dreams, but if she can't decide hypothetically between leather and suede at this stage, how many hours will you spend waiting for her in shoe shops while she deliberates over the real thing? Life's too short. Dump her now.

As well as simplifying everything, The Questions can also help dithering, indecisive individuals to cultivate better decision-making skills. Reaching quick, forceful conclusions not only makes you look good in a James Bond-ish sort of way (shaken or stirred? Does he ever hesitate?), it also eliminates many tedious discernments from your life. Take restaurant menus, for example. Why even look at the fruity puddings after you've firmly identified yourself as a confirmed brown pudding devotee?

The Questions often reveal our most hidden depths. Sometimes, these can be shocking as well as exciting, so if your beloved turns out to be a Creationist with a salted popcorn fetish, or you baulk at creating your future with a closet Cavalier, do not despair. You can survive this and make a wonderful life together by celebrating your differences. After all, someone has to eat the hard centres and you'll never need to fight over the window seat again. And if you're desperate for a flatmate who won't steal your Marmite, one simple Question could guarantee contentment and an untouched jar whenever you want it.

Once you're confident with the method, try keeping four or five favourite Questions handy for emergencies and don't be afraid to use them. If your job interview is going badly, just fire a quick "Greeks or Trojans?" at the boss. At best, this will give you both a wonderful new talking point and at worst, well, you didn't want to work there anyway, did you?

Here, then, are the keys to the relationships of your dreams. Use them wisely, perceptively and try not to take "don't know" for an answer.

Here we go.

Which do you prefer?

# The Questions

# Question 1

# Coke or Pepsi?

**COKE:** Let's start with what I think is the ultimate Question. It was the first one I ever came up with and believe me, it picks out the raisins from the muesli.

Coke was the original; it's not some Johnny-come-lately who tried to crib someone else's great idea. It's a winner. It taught the world to sing. Just ask Santa Claus – would he want a blue and white outfit? I don't think so.

And don't pretend you don't care, either. Tell me honestly – when you ask for a caramel-and-carbon-dioxide-based beverage, do you ever, ever say, "I'll have a Pepsi?" No, you always say, "I'll have a Coke" and sometimes the barman replies, "Er, will Pepsi do?" and then you look at each other, united for a moment in the miserable, mutual knowledge that really, it won't, but it's not his fault.

When you want to suck at the teat of Momma America, it has to be the real thing. **FM**


**PEPSI:** The cola individualist chooses Pepsi. Maybe it isn't that easy to taste the difference and, all things considered, it's simply a matter of choosing to suck at the *other* teat of Momma America, but Pepsi is the David to Coke's Goliath. It's the non-conformist choice, the rebel's choice – it's what the Jedi would drink, to stick two fingers up at the evil empire and its Coke-swigging stormtroopers. OK, so Pepsi sounds girly, and they employed the world's biggest pop star freak to endorse it, but PepsiCo has never been implicated in CIA attempts to overthrow Central American democracies. And what's more, at the moment you press your lips to the top of the Pepsi bottle, warm in the knowledge that all right-minded people will understand your little act of rebellion, you're also rewarded with sweet memories of Wham's loveliest backing singer. **WOL**

# Question 2

# Cats or dogs?

**CATS:** People say that cats are haughty, distant and ungrateful, and it's true. Cats look down on people, but this is because the ancient Egyptians once treated them as gods and they haven't forgotten it.

But I prefer cats because they remind me of women. The best kind of women. Owning a cat is the closest you can get to having Kristin Scott Thomas in your home. They have poise, grace, intelligence and they know they're lovely; they let you know how privileged you are to be allowed to stroke them for a while.

Dogs, on the other hand, are like little, hairy Bill Clintons. They love indiscriminately, drool over the furniture and rub their genitals on anything that moves. And then there's the hygiene problem. Is there any smell like it? Is there any word in any language that can adequately describe the stench of wet dog?

Cat people are dignified, chic intellectuals, who drink Pouilly Fuissé in book-lined studies and have far more important things to do than run around the house wiping slobber off the soft furnishings. Even if you aren't at all like this, people will assume you are, if you have a cat. **WOL**

**DOGS:** People who willingly choose cats over dogs are to be avoided at all costs. They are disloyal commitment-phobes with deep psychological scars that will never, ever heal. Why else would you pick an animal that can't love, hates being touched, scratches everything in sight (including you), coughs up fur balls, can't digest food properly and brings dead animals into the house? Dogs have no need to indulge in cheap mind games involving rotting flesh. They show their love in a straightforward way, by simply appreciating one's existence. They guide the blind, aid the deaf and don't need kitty-litter. It is a fact we must face – cat owners are people with issues and are unable to commit to any relationship. How many films have been made about a cat saving the world, or sitting by its owner's grave? None, that's how many. **CS**

# Question 3

# Star Wars or Star Trek?

**STAR WARS:** The human elements of the story are never submerged by the special effects and the plot revolves around a good/evil axis that's much more interesting than the pap served up at tedious *Trek* fests. We all know that the Federation represents a Republican White House – hence its obsession with invasion and flag waving.

The *Star Wars* ethic suggests that we all have courage and integrity, however ordinary we may seem, and it does not involve slapping other members of the galaxy about for no good reason. Darth Vader is a much scarier villain, with a far better name. And unless toilet paper in America is effective beyond all imagining, how did they ever think they could get away with calling their bad-guys Klingons? **CS**


**STAR TREK:** Beam me up, Scotty, and transport me with delight. My first love was James T. Kirk, but even now that wigs and corsets are no longer aphrodisiacs for me, I still love this show and its many incarnations. Where else can you get sturdy moral analysis of the human condition, deep cosmic philosophising, and polystyrene-based life-forms knocking the crap out of each other, all presented in fabulous, bite-sized Technicolor chunks?

If *Star Trek* is (supposedly) *Wagon Train* in space, then *Star Wars* is the bleedin' *Ring Cycle* and where's the fun in that? When I boldly go with Jim, Jean-Luc et al, I instantly feel better about Lycra, the Universe and Everything. *Star Trek* actually tells us something about ourselves. It's about people and humanity's more positive prospects. It's as much about friendships as it is about starships. *Star Trek* hopefully predicts a future where everybody on Earth (not some galaxy far, far away and long, long ago) has got together, shaken hands and is trying to make friends with the neighbours. In comparison, *Star Wars* is like some interminable old Icelandic saga, only dressed up in pretty pastels and much less literate. Remember Darth Maul, The Phantom Menace? Dennis the Menace was scarier. And let's not forget who was responsible for Jar Jar Binks. **FM**

# Question 4

# Christmas or Hogmanay?

**CHRISTMAS:** Presents! Shall I go on? Given the choice between a fun holiday with presents and a holiday with no presents, drunken vomiting and deep, inevitable depression about another year turning and having nothing to show for it, where's the problem?

Christmas is so exciting; it gives me a wonderful, warm feeling. Any warmth at Hogmanay is created accidentally, by the build-up of bodies in the drunken, seething crowds, full of beery-breathed yobs trying to stick their tongues down your throat. In fact, take away the drink, the crush and maybe the odd firework, and there's not much left.

I call Slade, Wizzard, Bing Crosby, and almost everybody else, from George Michael to John Lennon, as my witnesses. As you glide merrily through the enchanting, sparkling, pre-Christmas throng, remember that nobody ever wrote a heart-warming song called *New Year's Day*. U2 tried - and the dirge-like result almost makes you resolve never to see January 2nd. **FM**


**HOGMANAY:** Take out the worst bits of Christmas: the months spent agonising over buying presents, worrying about what useless tat you'll be given, pretending to like the tat you're given, pretending not to know everyone's pretending to like the tat you gave them. Take out the Queen's speech, the other rubbish on the telly, the visiting relatives, the bloody carol singers and the church service.

Now, take what you have left: the best bits – alcohol, food, no work – and add a few friends and some fireworks. This is Hogmanay.

On this night, the togetherness of humanity is at its most tangible. We wait as one, sharing the joy and anticipation of that same magical moment. The year turns…and you now have licence to snog whoever you like – with no recriminations! Local girls, girls on holiday, your mate's friend you always fancied. Attractive policewomen. Kiss them all.

I don't know the story behind it; I can only assume Hogman was some kind of Viking god, who drank and kissed lots of girls. Whatever; compared to this, Christ's day just doesn't do it for me. Hogman, whoever you were, you're the best. **WOL**

# Question 5

# Jaffa: cake or biscuit?

**CAKE:** Well it's called a Jaffa *Cake* by the people who make it, so that would be the main reason to think it's a cake. The other would be that, unlike a biscuit, it doesn't go soft when stale, but hard - a well-known cake characteristic. There's none so blind as those that call cakes 'biscuits'. **CS**


**BISCUIT:** For starters, they are small, flat, round things, covered in chocolate. This is a bit of a give-away, but ask yourself, when you go into the supermarket to buy your Jaffa Cakes, which aisle do you head for? Do you aim for the cakes and baked goods? No, you don't. You go straight to the biscuit section and lo, there they are.

Just because a thing is called 'cake' doesn't mean it is. Yellow cake is something you make Weapons of Mass Destruction out of, and good luck leaping out of a urinal cake at a Mafia birthday party. Don't let's get bogged down in semantics.

The real test comes when someone says to you: "Would you like a biscuit?" and produces a packet of Jaffa Cakes. All is well with the world. But imagine if they say: "Would you like some cake?" and you say: "Ooh, yes please" and they give you...a Jaffa Cake. It's not such a happy scenario, is it? Let's just accept that they're biscuits and start concentrating on the real question of whether the orangey bit in the middle is evil or not. **FM**

# Question 6

# EastEnders or
# Coronation Street?

**EASTENDERS:** *EastEnders* has more demanding storylines and is altogether a far more inventive soap. There are no awful Northern accents, no Vera Duckworth and no Ken Barlow. The acting is far better, too. *Corrie* has never yet reached the dramatic heights of the Den and Angie divorce, or the Sharon Watts love triangle. All *Corrie* can manage is a serial killer hiding behind a sofa (and don't tell me you weren't hoping he'd manage to top the chinless Gail Tilsley). Give me classy cockney, give me apples and pears, give me Dr Legg's eyebrows - but don't give me the camp that is *Corrie*. **CS**


**CORONATION STREET:** Interesting. Northern accents bother you, but you can sit for hours watching spade-faced Cockney fishwives screaming "Shatcha maaf yew cahhh!" at each other.
*Corrie* is wittier, pithier and far less pretentious. Because of its long history, it has a far greater awareness of its relative importance; it knows that its main function is to entertain, not to be *Panorama* with beer. This understanding has allowed it to develop good humour, superb characterisation and a healthy sense of the bizarre. *Corrie* characters are panto characters; everyone's done up to the nines, with gloriously unfeasible hairdos. Every time Richard Hillman appeared, you could barely stop yourself shouting out "He's behind you!"
*EastEnders* is full of miserable, mawkish mopers like Ian Beale, whose very presence makes self-immolation seem like a fun prospect. **WOL**

# Question 7

# Boxers or Y-fronts?

**BOXERS:** Since underwear became an issue for me (i.e. when it began to involve women), I have worn boxers. The shift away from Y-fronts began when my Gran bought me a pair of *Scooby-Doo* Y-fronts for Christmas 1973. They looked ridiculous, and my sister's constant teasing planted the germ of my hatred for Y-fronts (but not for Daphne from the *Scooby-Doo* gang). I'll never be able to thank my sister enough for this. Boxers are air conditioned, comfortable and don't look like something Reg Varney would have worn in *On the Buses*. Y-fronts are comedy pants. Boxers are worn by heroes. You can bet Fred wore boxers and Shaggy wore Y-fronts. Daphne always went with Fred, ergo…
It's the difference between getting laid and checking in at the nearest monastery. **WOL**


**Y-FRONTS:** If a bloke wears Y-fronts, you know that he's completely his own man – totally secure and comfortable with his inner-underwear. It's like he's saying, "I'm an unfettered male animal. I can wear unfashionable pants and still overpower you with my raw masculinity. No poncey male model in white boxers is going to tell my boys where to nestle".
It's also true that Y-fronts give a girl a much better idea of what's on offer. They create an appealing, Linford Christie effect, whereas boxers tell you nothing, except maybe when they were last washed.
Aidan in *Sex and the City* was a Y-front man, so that's all we need to know. **FM**

# Question 8

# Monopoly or Scrabble?

**MONOPOLY:** So much less effort and so much more money! It's like being Donald Trump without the problem hair. You can own hotels in Mayfair, learn financial acumen and quite a bit of geography, too. I can't tell you how excited I was the first time I went to the Angel, Islington, because it's my favourite cheap property.

Monopoly always makes me happy - so long as I can be the Scottie dog - and it's the only game in which I've ever won a beauty contest, so it must be good.

Scrabble players are so anal. Always running off to check the dictionary and crowing over their fifty point bonuses. They're both serious and superior at the same time - never a good combination when you're supposed to be having fun. **FM**


**SCRABBLE:** Scrabble is simply marvellous. It enables you to widen your vocabulary and have fun with tiles. It can also be an unusual tool in your seduction kit. Light a few candles, put on some soft music, whip out your Scrabble board and get the object of your desire to play the rude version with you. You'll be in each other's arms before you can say "Triple word score".

Monopoly is rubbish. If you don't land on Mayfair, you don't stand a chance; it goes on for days; spreads capitalist propaganda and one of the counters is an iron. How crap is that? **CS**

# Question 9

# Tea or coffee?

**TEA:** The choice of the civilised world. Tea was first drunk by the great, ancient Eastern cultures; the ones that gave us the best philosophy, meditation and the most creative sexual positions. Thanks to the invincibility of tea, these civilisations survived destruction because their invaders also fell in love with the thinking-man's brew. Nowadays, the decent, democratic tea-drinking world holds out against the evil, corporate, high-rise, coffee-drinking world, which sprang from brutally successful invasions of gun-powderless cultures, most of which preferred cocoa anyway.

Tea must be a gift from the Gods because how else could Ancient Man have looked at a simple, unassuming leaf and thought, "Hmm, if I pick that, dry it, shred it, boil it in water and serve it with scones, it wouldn't half make a nice little earner in the Cotswolds"? Tea isn't just the builder of great empires, it's a direct link to the transcendental. When you've had an accident, lost the love of your life, or just bought a packet of Rich Tea, does anybody ever say, "There, there, come in, sit down and have a cup of jitter-juice"? No, because only tea makes everything better. **FM**


**COFFEE:** Coffee is my lifeblood, my *raison d'être*. It is the only reason to get up and face the joyless hell that is the working day. The magical melding of ground bean, water and milk is beverage alchemy.

Having left the safety of the sheets, only that first cup of coffee can defend you against the assault of those early morning quandaries, torturing you about the state of your life and the total lack of sanity on the planet. With the sudden caffeine high, gloom is dispersed and all is right with the world. Anyone who doesn't understand this needs to be cut out of your life, or certainly your mornings. Tea is simply not cool and doesn't jump start the heart. **CS**

# Question 10

# Best or Beckham?

**BEST:** George Best was football's first media superstar. He was so popular at one point, he was getting thousands of fan letters every week. His floppy-mop hair was so distinctive, and so frequently copied by fans, that he became known as 'the fifth Beatle'. Nowadays, this is all part and parcel of the top-flight football scene, but it all started with George and for a very good reason. He was an absolute, no-holds-barred, jaw-droppingly fantastic football genius. He was so great, Pele named him as his favourite player.

Yes, George has his faults – with his penchant for booze and bankruptcy - but he's always retained a sense of humility and was never too precious to turn out for the likes of the San Jose Earthquakes, Dunstable Town and Ford Open Prison.

The tragedy of George Best is that he could have been even better than he was; Beckham's tragedy is that he will never be as good as everyone thinks he is. Yes, Beckham's free kicks are good, but he is a mincing catwalk dandy compared to Best. **WOL**


**BECKHAM:** As far as I'm concerned, being asked to prefer one ex-Manchester United player to another is a choice between the Red Devils and the deep blue sea. It pains my heart even to enter the debate, but every Question demands an answer and mine is Beckham. OK, he sometimes looks like the fairy on the Christmas tree, and I'm never going to defend the Alice-band, but even if his reputation as a good family man has been questioned, nobody ever played away as much as Best.

I will forever admire the fact that, despite the demands of his profession, Beckham had the courage to marry a brunette. Best's bleach-blindness means he can never see past a woman's peroxide follicles. Assuming, of course, he can see past the bottom of his glass.

Beckham must also be congratulated for knowing when the hell to get away from MU – always the biggest plus in any footballer's career – and even I can see that when he shoots, he usually scores.

Two golden balls, one wife, one liver, no convictions. Beckham must be best. **FM**

# Question 11

# Cavaliers or Roundheads?

**CAVALIERS**: Almost all of us are closet Cavaliers, because although we deem it politically correct to plump for the warty ones, we would secretly prefer to be clad in silky tunics and look terribly dashing. The Cavaliers were fearsome soldiers with a wardrobe to match - proving it's perfectly possible to be macho and carry off a frilly shirt. Cromwell had ultimate power, made his son successor and found Parliament impossible (sounds familiar). Lord Protector? Lord protect *us* more like. He banned Christmas, dancing and the need for wigs. It took Charles II to restore Britain's much needed sartorial elegance and *joie de vivre*. The Roundheads were clearly not as much fun, certainly not as comely and were no doubt crap in bed. **CS**


**ROUNDHEADS:** No, we're certainly not all closet Cavaliers. There's no way I'd have fought for anyone but the New Model Army (and by the way, how cool does that sound?). The Roundheads were the first working-class, professional army and they completely gubbed the gentlemen amateurs in their wildly inappropriate, dressing-up box gear. The Roundheads were leather and iron — manly and tough. The Cavaliers were lace and velvet and Daddy's best sword, which thankfully was no match for a Roundhead pike.

Nobody expected the common upstarts to win against a king's army, but they did and ushered in the greatest period of prosperity England had known for years. I don't want sartorial elegance; I want balanced books and fair taxation. Calm, Commonwealth satisfaction wins over orgiastic, Restoration carousing. And who wants wigs?

Remember, "Don't be so cavalier" is always an admonishment. Nobody ever gets criticised for having a Roundhead attitude to life, because deep down, everybody knows that a Cavalier is a bad thing - and so is a frilly shirt. **FM**

# Question 12

# Pudding:
# fruity or brown?

**FRUITY:** Fruit-based puddings, of whatever sort, are not usually so rich, so consequently you are able to eat much more of them before feeling sick as a dog. Whilst munching your way through your third helping of fruits-of-the-forest Pavlova, you can easily con yourself into believing that what you are shoving into your gob is vaguely healthy. It involves fruit, for God's sake.

Brown puddings – essentially the chocolate family and all its monotonously beige relatives – are so limited. Choosing brown also means shutting the door on raspberry flan and apple crumble and I, for one, am not prepared to do that without a struggle. Last but not least, the fruity option is always more aesthetically pleasing, as it can never resemble a nasty bowel accident. **CS**


**BROWN:** So you've munched your way, quietly and dutifully, through a course or two of 'good' food, with vitamins and fibres and whatnot. These probably included vegetables – maybe even *steamed* vegetables. But you made it through and arrived at the final destination. Indeed, the whole objective of any meal is to arrive at this point – pudding. Yum, you think, here is my reward for stoical perseverance. But what's this? Fruit? *On* the pudding? *In* the pudding? *Is* the pudding?

In God's name, why?

Pudding is about pleasure - it's a reward, a treat. Therefore all puddings are good, but fruity pudding is only an option if there is no other option. Brown puddings always outrank fruity ones because you know this is the proper, no-holds-barred pudding experience. There's no risk of finding roughage in your crème caramel, or an unwanted dash of vitamin C in your chocolate fudge cake. So, away with the mango mousse and apple pie; bring on the brown: butterscotch, chocolate, caramel, toffee, coffee, fudge, treacle…these are the stuff of real puddings, these are my just reward. **WOL**

# Question 13

# Animals or children?

**ANIMALS:** Far more rewarding and cheaper to maintain. Keeping animals doesn't render you incapable of having a conversation that doesn't revolve around nappies, teething, or the local education system. Also, animals don't go through any recognisable adolescence, so there are no Freudian ties that need to be severed. You're spared spotty confusion on their part and feelings of failure on yours. Do yourself a favour and choose something that requires less upkeep and less strain on your bank account. **CS**


**CHILDREN:** A dog is OK for fifteen years or so, but it won't keep you in your old age. I want the fruit of my loins to go forth, prosper, make the world a better place and then look after me in my dotage, because I don't have a pension plan. Also, while you can train dogs and monkeys to do tricks, a child can be taught to carry out extremely sophisticated tasks, like begging to go to Disneyland, which suits me fine as I've been looking for an excuse to go there for years. **WOL**

# Question 14

# World Wars:
# First or Second?

**FIRST:** It's the only war in the history of mankind to be called "great". It really was The Great War. It had great poetry, great guns, great battle names (Passchendaele and Meuse-Argonne to name but two), it had a great flower and by far the greatest uniforms. It was a great, big sprawling mess of a war; the precursor of great social and military change and most significant of all, it was the great lesson that history ignored. **CS**


**SECOND:** It's in colour. **FM**

# Question 15

# Batman or Spiderman?

**BATMAN:** He's a self-made man/bat. He's just a rich bloke who decided to become a superhero, which is taking philanthropy about as far as it can go. Think about it. Bruce Wayne uses all his wealth, intelligence and strength to one end – the destruction of evil. He could have spent his whole life lounging around his big house teasing his butler, but no, he chose to combat crime and flash his six-pack in defence of the city he loves.

The most inspirational thing about Batman is that good men everywhere can actually aspire to be him. All you need is a profound sense of justice and a knack with a toolkit and lo, those great gadgets - and even the cool car - can be yours. Batman proves that you don't need to be from an alien planet, or bitten by a radioactive spider, to be a superhero. You, too, can combat the forces of organised crime, so long as you're righteous to the core and have great pecs. **FM**

**SPIDERMAN:** Spiderman is an organic superhero. The real thing. He doesn't have to pop home to collect the car before he goes out to do good. He has actual powers, including the awesome ability to shoot webs out of unexpected orifices. Peter Parker is genetically modified to fight crime; he's not just playing at fancy dress. Batman is totally reliant on his gadgets - take them away and he's Bill Gates in black tights. Spidey is an ordinary guy, with neither money nor social status to bolster his self-esteem. He's a self-contained superhero who doesn't need help from some pretty-boy sidekick whose powers, one can only assume from his name, include the ability to tap through milk bottle tops. **WOL**

# Question 16

# Sun or moon?

**SUN:** The only moon I've ever had any time for was Keith.
There's a reason people sleep all night and it's not just because you can't get a tan from the moon. The sun is the centre of everything; the bringer of life, light and vitamin D. It's how man likes to see himself; the main attraction, the source of all power, the big ego in the sky. When the sun is out, people do more and when it's hot, women wear less. **WOL**


**MOON:** The moon is so subtle and mysterious. Nothing clandestine, or breathtakingly romantic, is ever done by sunlight. Nor did Oberon and Titania arrange their ill-meeting for midday and for good reason, because the sun is so relentless, so crass and so very, very yellow.
The delicate, silvery luminosity of a full moon has an exciting, yet enigmatic quality, brimming with suggestion. The moon controls the tide, and so exudes a primal, magnetic power that the sun doesn't have. It also allows couples to court, won't give you cancer, age you prematurely or encourage people to serve you a salad. **CS**

# Radio Times or TV Times?

**RADIO TIMES:** *TV Times* is for people who want to know what's on television. *Radio Times* is for people who want to know *about* television. It's an institution in its own right; an in-depth, intelligent read and a proud, but fair, torchbearer for the Corporation. And nothing on this earth can beat the glorious anticipation of picking up the Christmas double issue of *Radio Times* and sitting down with a cup of tea and a marker pen. Bliss! But even if it had none of these fine qualities, *Radio Times* would still give me something that no other magazine does properly - the most vital and absorbing complement to any serious television habit - lovely, long, detailed cast and credits lists. **FM**


**TV TIMES:** The point of *both* publications is to let you know what's on television, although the *Radio Times* certainly does this in a more up-market way than its plebeian rival. The *TV Times* is a cheap, brash, sensation-seeking affair, which means it is a far more accurate and honest representation of what you will experience if you actually watch the television. The *Radio Times* is a very well turned-out madam, but she's still trying to get you to sleep with a pox-ridden tart. **WOL**

# Question 18

# Freud or Jung?

**FREUD:** Freud (pronounced 'Frood' in America) is one of those icons of Western civilisation you just have to take your hat off to. At possibly the most prudish time in history, he burst on to the stage saying "It's all about sex! What men really want is to kill their fathers and sleep with their mothers!" This must have terrified the sort of gentlemen who hardly dared utter the word 'titillate' without worrying that the ladies present would faint and they'd be banished in disgrace, to live out the rest of their lives in the French Foreign Legion.

His answer to everything was "It's about sex", or "It's about the repression of sex". He was the Benny Hill of Viennese academia.

Most men know that Freud was right (apart from the Oedipus thing). We think about sex about twenty times an hour and sometimes get turned on even when we're not thinking about sex. Girls, whenever you say "What are you thinking about?" and we reply "Oh, nothing", the real answer, which Freud knew, is that we're thinking about sex. What are you thinking about? **WOL**


**JUNG:** How about archetypes, synchronicity, introversion, extroversion, lucid dreaming, word association and the collective unconscious? Jung was too busy thinking about these to get all hot under the collar. But what I like most about Jung is that he's so flexible, so much more open to possibilities. Granted, he's got Freud's work as a jumping-off point, but away he goes into the wide, blue realms of mythology and spirituality, while old Sigmund is still stuck on his couch, rigidly insisting that if you dream about banana splits, you need help.

Yet the best example of why I'd choose Jung over Freud dates back to 1909, when they were passing the time on a train journey by analysing each other's dreams. Jung was having a great time, but Freud suddenly refused to play the game any more. Apparently, he felt he was losing his authority. Too late for that already, Siggy baby. **FM**

# Question 19

# Cosmonaut or astronaut?

**COSMONAUT:** First man in space, first woman in space, first animal in space, longest stay in space – all cosmonauts. You don't have to flounce about on the moon to be a proper spaceman, but Americans are obliged to go on and on about their moon landings, because that's the only time the Russians didn't get there first.

Russia didn't have America's money, or its technology, but their space programme stole such a march on the US, NASA was forced to take a larger step than it might otherwise have done. So, in a way, the USSR should also be congratulated for inspiring the first moon landing. Either way, cosmonauts win.

I love the word, too. Cosmonaut: universal sailor. It's so much more ambitious, more exciting, than a mere astronaut – star sailor. Why confine yourself to the stars, when there's a whole universe out there? **FM**


**ASTRONAUT:** Well they might not have been the first in space, but they were the first to take that giant step and that's what counts. The comrades might be universal sailors, but their little universal sailor feet were not the first to collect moon dust. I'm sure the cosmonauts were firing their pets into the sky for years, but it took an astronaut to turn up, see what needed to be done and just flippin' well do it. **CS**

# Question 20

# Hanging or beheading?

**HANGING:** We're talking doing, not watching, right? Well I'd choose hanging every time. If cowboy films teach us anything, it's that there's always a chance you can survive a hanging. If you've made some kind of arrangement beforehand, Clint Eastwood will expertly sever the rope with a single shot, then you leap on a horse, ride away and share the reward money he got for turning you in.

Beheading is way too close to the bone and so final. You can only survive a beheading for a few moments and that's only when the executioner fails first time around, leaving you running about with your head half-off, until he finishes the job. No thanks. Anyway, with hanging, there's the possibility for some kind of autoerotic experience, which would be a small compensation for being put to death. **WOL**


**BEHEADING:** So much cleaner! What's more, beheading attracts a much better class of condemned. Anybody can be dragged out of bed and lynched from the nearest tree with no ceremony at all, but a proper beheading takes planning. Occasionally, headsmen have to be brought from foreign climes, or the condemned asks for a practise block to get their death just right. It's a perfectionist's way to go. Yes, it's a tad final, but if you accept your fate, it's much more refined than having your eyes pop out and your tongue loll everywhere as you hang from a dirty rope for days, until the carrion get you.

Give me a nice, low-cut dress, my hair up, a good crowd and I'm ready for my close-up now, Monsieur Guillotine. **FM**

# Question 21

# Bath or shower?

**BATH:** No shower is a pleasure. It means you have to be somewhere quickly - usually work. A bath gives scope for relaxation, contemplation and the idle perusal of one's genitals. Great thoughts come to those who bathe. There is no record of anybody ever coming up with a decent mathematical theorem in the shower. But the best thing about a bath is that you don't have to do anything. You just lie there and suddenly, you're clean. **WOL**


**SHOWER:** Showers are swift, efficient, invigorating and don't leave you sitting in your own filth. I really don't want to contemplate my ever-increasing navel and I'm already much more intimate with my body than I want to be. Because only half of me can remain warm at any one time, it's impossible to stay put long enough to make the whole effort worthwhile. Baths are a waste of water, hard to clean, impossible to wash your hair in and much more difficult to share. **CS**

# Question 22

# Window seat or aisle seat?

**WINDOW SEAT:** Get out of my way! There is nothing, *nothing* worse in this world than the vile scabs of humanity who take the window seat and then proceed to read a book. Window seats are for adventurers, open-minded children of nature, who actually want to see what's going on beyond ends of their noses. I seem to spend my life craning to see past idiots who are too absorbed in *The Celestine Prophecy* to notice that there's a world out there and they're making me miss it.

Any journey away from the window seat is a nightmare of tedium, but on a plane, it's very hell. I need to see everything. If I can't see the ground, I want to see the clouds. It's all so hugely interesting, don't you think? You can even plot the route with a map.

Aisle seats are dull, dull, dull and if you prefer them, you're my hero. **FM**


**AISLE SEAT:** When travelling on aeroplanes with a girlfriend, I have always found that she would prefer the window seat. But I never say, "You have the window seat, I know you prefer it". Instead, I wait until she asks if she can have the window seat and then intimate that I, too, would normally like the window seat, but being a gentleman, I'm happy to let her have it. On both the outward and return journeys. My girlfriends have always been grateful for my generosity in this. They do not know that I am actually perfectly happy in the aisle seat, which offers greater leg-room and a far superior view of the air hostesses as they sashay up and down the plane. **WOL**

# Question 23

# Rugby or soccer?

**RUGBY:** The players are better looking, don't have such naff haircuts, don't spit as much, don't wear jewellery and don't pretend to be injured the whole time. The supporters are not malingerers, hooligans or faux London wide-boys educated at Eton, and the managers are not ill-assorted European riff raff out to make a swift buck. It is a sport where the game is more important than the money, we occasionally win a major international tournament and the offside rule isn't nearly so complicated. **CS**


**SOCCER:** Soccer has been with mankind ever since Homo erectus first slammed a skull past the Neanderthal goalie, straight into the cave mouth, and ran around hugging his mates. The development of man is in direct correlation to the development of football, which is why every nation on earth aspires to be recognised as the cradle of the beautiful game. It's part of Planet Earth's identity and when the Martians land, we won't take them seriously until they join Fifa. No public schoolboy picking up a football and running with it, because he can't make the soccer first team, is ever going to change the magic and mystery that is the bond between man and his big, round ball. **WOL**

# Question 24

# Spring and autumn or summer and winter?

**SPRING AND AUTUMN:** The journey is so much more interesting than the destination and Mother Nature agrees with me. The beautiful, delicate greens of spring confirm that the dull, damp, depressing winter is over and we're finally free from tinsel, *Only Fools and Horses* and mince pies. Similarly, the gorgeous reds and yellows of autumn let us know that the dusty, horrible summer is finally at an end and we can breathe easily again. This proves that travelling to the extremes of summer and winter looks better, smells better and *is* better than actually getting there. **CS**


**SUMMER AND WINTER:** All extremes are good. Big heat and big cold, that's what I want. All the wet, misty, mushy bits in between are way too unsatisfactory and non-committal. Don't give me any half-measures; let me bake and freeze. In an ideal world, I'd wake up one morning after six months of wearing polar fleece and think, yes! Bikini time!

The solstices have always been tremendously important to mankind, going right back to the days when the last word in entertainment was watching the sun go up and down. Neolithic man didn't build Stonehenge because he fancied an equinox party.

And as far as holidays are concerned, you can't beat summer and Christmas, so spare me the middle-men and let's cut to the main attractions. **FM**

# Question 25

# Brad Pitt or Johnny Depp?

**BRAD PITT:** I'd definitely have kicked Brad out of bed for appearing in a Guy Ritchie movie, but I can't help liking him, partly because he didn't build his career out of finding ways to look cool. I think he probably just is.

Anybody who can make fourteen minutes of screen time into an unforgettable showcase, as Brad did in *Thelma and Louise*, gets my vote and let's face it, until he came along with his six-pack of iron, a lot of Hollywood's leading men had really let themselves go.

However, what I like best about him is his wife. Brad had the courage to marry a real woman, with talents at least equal to his. Unlike many of Tinseltown's finest, he isn't so insecure that he can't live with anyone who doesn't look and sound like a kitten. **FM**


**JOHNNY DEPP:** Mr Pitt is the manifestation of everything bad about film stars: he's blond, a mouth-breather and has the acting ability of a courgette. He takes himself far too seriously and you can tell that he considers himself talented. Well, mister, I've seen *Troy* and I'm not so sure.

By contrast, Mr Depp is intelligent and gifted. He makes unusual, eclectic films and doesn't need to whip his kit off in order to impress his legions of fans. He is quirky, funny and has the mouth of a Greek god; the man can marry a whole damn zoo as far as I'm concerned. **CS**

# Question 26

# USA or Canada?

**UNITED STATES:** The extreme nature of the States does mean it has many unsavoury aspects, but when you weigh them up against the literature, art and humour it has produced, they are a price worth paying. Canada never created *Frasier*, *Hill Street Blues*, Arthur Miller or anything worth bothering about. Indeed, on reflection, I can't see any point to it at all, other than as a place to wear a lumberjack shirt.

America even has New York, a metropolis so magnificent they wrote a million songs about it. No one ever sang "Ottawa, Ottawa, so good they named it twice". Canadian cities have never inspired anybody. Why would they? The whole country's just too damned boring. **CS**


**CANADA:** To avoid attack from disaffected peoples across the globe, lots of American travellers put the Canadian flag on their backpacks and pretend to be Canadian. Canadians don't need to pretend to be anything other than what they are: the proud owners of real mountains, real wilderness and real Mounties, resplendent in the best uniforms of any police force, anywhere in the world.

Canada also gave us Elliot Gould, Leonard Cohen and Shania Twain (yum). Quietly superior to their loudmouth cousins across the border, they get on with their seal culling and don't bother anyone. Most Canadians even know where Europe is. **WOL**

# Question 27

# The Beatles or the Stones?

**THE BEATLES:** One of my two least favourite Questions of all time. Why do people persist in asking it? Isn't the answer the epitome of the bleedin' obvious?

OK, then: The Beatles were perfect. And everything the Beatles did perfectly, the Stones tried to copy, usually tediously and always about three months later. No sane person prefers *Their Satanic Majesties Request* to *Sergeant Pepper*. Assuming they've heard of it.

The Beatles will never be surpassed. They are the Shakespeares of modern music, rightly beloved across the - I nearly said 'universe' - globe for saying it all; beautifully. There are no words to praise them highly enough, so I'll stop trying, but God knows, I'd rather listen to the worst, rejected Ringo track ever (*If You've Got Trouble*) than *Jumping Jack Flash*.

The Stones only ever get mentioned in the same breath as the Beatles (who gave the Stones their first single, so maybe they weren't all good) because people hate to admit that something can be entirely in a class of its own. But the Beatles are, so accept it.

The Stones or the Monkees? Now, there's a Question. Definitely the Monkees. **FM**


**THE ROLLING STONES:** Although less good looking, the Stones managed to be miles sexier, had far better girlfriends and seemed to have much more fun. Initially, their songs were earthier and more adult than the Beatles' pop tunes and they didn't endlessly bang on about flying high with some old strawberries. When the Stones sang about drugs, it didn't make me wish I'd taken them first. Even better, because they didn't try so hard to be experimental or clever, there were no eighteen-hour-long songs or weird sound effects to contend with. I could just relax and enjoy the music. Fortunately, the Stones had the sense not to go too deeply into mysticism, so Mick et al didn't insist on loving everyone. Yoko really didn't arrive a moment too soon. **CS**

# Question 28

# Napoleon or Wellington?

**NAPOLEON:** My other least favourite Question.

Can you really compare a man who brought liberty to much of Europe, led the world's most superb army and created the greatest empire since Charlemagne out of nothing - to a man who had one lucky afternoon? No, but morons still ask this Question.

It's sacrilege to equate them at all, but as statesmen it's impossible. Napoleon's brilliance was unparalleled. He was self-made and rose by his own merits to be voted emperor by an adoring nation. Wellesley became Prime Minister on the back of his so-called victory at Waterloo, made a hash of it, arrogantly loathed the commoners and they paid him back by smashing all his windows.

As soldiers, comparison is almost as pointless. Even I can't deny that Napoleon lost Waterloo, but Wellesley certainly didn't win it. He was all but defeated when the Prussians arrived to save him and his entire reputation is built on pure luck. In Spain, he was extremely lucky to avoid fighting Napoleon. The one time they met on the battlefield, he got lucky again and that's the only reason we remember him.

Napoleon is immortal for twenty years of pure genius, not a few hours of good fortune. And boy, he looked good on the coins. **FM**


**WELLINGTON:** For all that he was cold, distant, egotistical and reactionary, Wellington's talents were not insignificant. He learnt from his early mistakes in India and became a master of the 'reverse slope' tactic (in other words, 'hide behind the hill so the cannons can't get you'), an approach that ultimately helped rob Napoleon of victory at Waterloo.

Although he never fought Napoleon's best marshals in Spain, he did win the Peninsular War, despite the hindrance of inept fellow British officers and his useless and duplicitous allies, the Spanish. Later in life, he was an unpopular and ultra-conservative Prime Minister, yet he was responsible for the unusually progressive step of securing Catholic Emancipation in Ireland – a worthwhile achievement in itself. Overall, perhaps Napoleon was the better man, the better military leader, the better politician and the more modern, progressive human being, but he failed himself and his country when it mattered most. **WOL**

# Question 29

# Strawberries or raspberries?

**STRAWBERRIES:** The King of the Berries. The biggest berry, the brightest berry, the best berry. It pushes past the other, lesser berries to take its rightful place on the throne of Berrydom. It's the only one with the seeds on the outside (not necessarily a recommendation, but certainly a distinction) and maybe because of this wanton display of fertility, the strawberry is also the sensual berry. No girl ever got turned on by the thought of being fed chocolate-dipped raspberries. There's no point, because they're too fiddly, too mushy and they don't go well with champagne. If you're ever on *Family Fortunes*, and Les Dennis asks you to name a berry, don't think twice. Go straight for the strawberry, because it will always be the first berry the general public think of. Apart, perhaps, from Halle. **WOL**


**RASPBERRIES:** Raspberries are the gastronomic manifestation of summer. These small bundles of intense flavour are not as ubiquitous as their rival, so their appeal is more potent. They are less pretentious than strawberries and, because they don't have a paltry, lacklustre flavour, they don't need to be enhanced by expensive champagne. They can be used far more effectively in tarts and on shortbread, as they aren't so big and ungainly. What's more, raspberries can give you hours of fun. Come on now, when was the last time you blew a strawberry at someone? **CS**

# Question 30

# Tits or bums?

**TITS:** Typical. The man says tits. Well, I must say I surprised myself here, because I really do like a nice bum and long legs (my favourite part of the female anatomy is the curve where bum and leg meet). A great chest could never make up for a bad bum and short legs.

So why do I champion tits? Well, the problem with bums is that everyone has them. There is nothing exclusively womanly about the bottom. I once saw a website where there were twenty bottoms and you had to guess which were male and which were female (made more difficult by the fact that the men were trying to make their bottoms look womanly). I didn't get them all right.

You know that embarrassing moment when you see a lovely bosom then look up, only to realise you've been ogling a man? No? That's because *it can't happen*. Tits are a woman-only thing; once you establish the presence of breasts, you are generally safe to proceed. **WOL**


**BUMS:** Bums are aesthetically pleasing, give you something to get hold of and form the basis for the whole body. A good bottom can be likened to a split atom – a cleaved whole that forms two beautiful spheres of firm flesh. A perfect example of yin and yang; one cheek is useless without the other. So, it's not just something to sit on, but a whole philosophy. A great arse is a thing of beauty - think Michelangelo's *David* and, well, just keep on thinking. **CS**

# Question 31

# Hero or anti-hero?

**HERO:** When Bonnie Tyler sang *I'm Holding Out For A Hero*, she said it all, as far as I'm concerned. But as Bonnie quite rightly lamented, thoroughly good men are thin on the ground these days. If there's a Hercules, or a white knight on his fiery steed out there, then come on down. I don't like my heroes to be too complicated. I want a confident, capable, good guy; not some scummy, haunted type who's too busy struggling with his dark side to beat the bad guys properly. There's nothing wrong with simply being good and fighting for your rights. An anti-hero is usually no more than yet another bad guy surrounded by even worse guys. Just do the job, for God's sake and spare us your tortured soul.

Like Bonnie, I'm holding out for a real hero – preferably strong, preferably fast and it never hurts to be fresh from the fight. **FM**


**ANTI-HERO:** Far sexier, far more complex and therefore far more interesting; such men tend to become significant in spite of themselves. An anti-hero is motivated by intrinsically human emotions, like power, sex, money, or the need to exorcise the inner-demons haunting his sexy ass. Who wants some God-like knucklehead, all sweaty and horrible from the fight? Not this chick, that's for sure. I want a man out of his time; I want him to push limits and change the world, not simply save it with blind muscle-power. I want Marlon Brando in *The Wild One*, Holden Caulfield, or Clint Eastwood's Man with No Name; someone whose tormented brilliance blazes a new trail for future generations. That's the sort of hero I'm holding on for, not some walking six-pack with a lust for glory. **CS**

# Question 32

# Army: Salvation or Territorial?

**SALVATION ARMY:** Nobody gets killed; everybody gets soup. It's a more elite outfit than the TA because it demands both physical *and* spiritual commitment. Nobody's being paid to dress up and play the tuba; they're doing it for love, not for the promise of namby-pamby bonding weekends in Camberley, or the occasional jolly to Belize. The Sally Army mean business. They're part-time, they're unpaid, and they firmly believe that they're fighting the *good* fight, not just someone else's. And anyway, when was the last time the TA brightened up anyone's miserable Christmas shopping trip? **WOL**


**TERRITORIAL ARMY:** Soup and good intentions are all very well, but if we're invaded, I'm not sure that waving some smoked haddock chowder at the enemy will really cut it, frankly. The Territorials might hurl themselves about the Home Counties at the weekend, but if that means they're prepared to kill the baddies I, for one, am not going to stop them. They don't try and convert me; they don't make me listen to a brass band; they have better uniforms and my vote. **CS**

# Question 33

**Bumps in the night:
stay in bed or
get up and investigate?**

**STAY IN BED:** Many thousands of years ago, our ancestors would go out hunting. They would scout around looking for animals to trap, spear and kill. Sometimes they would come across a cave and suddenly, a deep, blood-curdling growl would resound from within. Our ancestors were the ones who ran away, or at least camped a safe distance away until whatever was in the cave came out. No doubt, though, there would be some idiot hominid who said, "I'll just pop into the cave and see what it is. You wait here." That was natural selection. This question is the same thing in a contemporary setting. Going to investigate is a form of suicide. The only safe course of action is to remain in bed and pull the covers up to your chin. **WOL**


**GET UP AND INVESTIGATE:** What's the matter with you? Get out there and save yourself, your family and your home from certain disaster. Be brave – and take a large poker. You're not going to meet a sabre-toothed tiger. The worst that could happen is that you'll thwack some thug in a Burberry-print baseball cap into the next life and get a short, but celebrated sentence. Your family, friends and the *Daily Mail* will all stand by you and you'll have a book deal when you come out. At best, all you'll find is that a painting fell off the wall, but that shouldn't stop you telling everyone you fought off several heavily-armed, masked attackers single-handed. You might still get that book deal. **FM**

# Question 34

# Sainsbury's or Tesco?

**SAINSBURY'S:** You only have to look at who they chose to endorse their stores to know which to plump for. Sainsbury's went for a young, hip, über-chef with a passion for food; Tesco opted for Prunella Scales' tight-fisted granny. I know which image I'm aspiring to, as I merrily wheel my trolley between the chargrilled artichokes and the Sancerre every Saturday morning. The feisty, zesty orange of Sainsbury's says entertaining; it says come in and look at our enormously well stocked wine section; it says National Gallery; it says rule, Britannia! **CS**


**TESCO:** I like Tesco. It's cheaper (allegedly). And don't forget the Air Miles. **FM**

# Question 35

# Hamlet or Macbeth?

**HAMLET:** This question sorts the thinkers from the doers. *Hamlet* is all about prevarication and indecision - well, welcome to my world. I can relate far more easily to a protagonist who would rather contemplate his own death than organise someone else's. Macbeth is one big knee-jerk reaction in a kilt, hasn't an original thought in his head and takes advice from several clearly unstable women without a murmur. At least Ophelia had the grace to lose it totally before handing out a load of crap advice about killing the king.

*Hamlet* explores the fundamental issue, our reason for being on this earth. It might be a long evening, but those of us with an attention span longer than a goldfish's are richly rewarded by a play that ends with a resounding bang. Hamlet fulfils his destiny with style and panache, unlike the hallucinating Scot, who turns out to be all mouth and no doublet and hose. **CS**


**MACBETH:** It's half as long. And they crack on with it - no mooning about with flower-laden bints. If anyone had killed Macbeth's dad and rogered his mum, he'd be mincemeat by the end of Act One. Half the deaths in *Hamlet* are accidental. In *Macbeth*, it's all deliberate and that's very satisfying. The girl's better, too. **WOL**

# Question 36

# Dracula or
# Frankenstein's Monster?

**DRACULA:** Tall, dark, aristocratic. He has excellent teeth and his breath never smells of garlic. The Count is a sexual force, able to transform prissy Victorian heroines into women who can't say "no". Dracula makes base, physical desires manifest; he is the seductive face of evil and I find this fascinating. He can only sleep on his native soil, casts no shadow, can appear in a mist, or as an animal, and has no reflection. What a guy! I find him so much more compelling than the boring, wimpy, self-pitying monster. Now he really *is* a pain in the neck. **CS**


**FRANKENSTEIN'S MONSTER:** Aw, bless! He's just an innocent lunk abroad, isn't he? I've got no sympathy for Dracula because he knows the score, but he still keeps on making trouble for himself. He hasn't even got the sense to wear a watch. The poor Monster didn't ask to be born and he certainly didn't ask to be put in a suit ten sizes too small. What kind of parenting is that, Dr Frankenstein?

The odds are unfairly stacked against the Monster. He wants to make friends, but everybody either runs towards him with flaming torches and pitchforks, or runs away from him screaming. Anybody that stays always gets accidentally killed - usually by him. Even his girlfriend turned out to be a right bitch. He never really had a chance, but despite the odds, he always tries the make the best of things. He's a good guy – with bolts. **FM**

# Question 37

# Cricket: Test match or 20/20?

**TEST MATCH:** This is like comparing a long and happy marriage with a one night stand. Test match cricket is by far the more rewarding of the two; it just requires a little patience. It takes time for the teams to suss each other out, for the players to work out how best to employ their own strengths and exploit their opponents' weaknesses. It's so much more interesting to watch a match that's as much a psychological contest as a physical one, and if this takes a little more time, then I, for one, am in it for the duration.

When Test wickets are taken, or runs made, the atmosphere is incredibly exciting and can stay at fever pitch for days. 20/20 is very much a wham-bam-thank-you-ma'am experience, with none of the foreplay necessary for a truly good time. It's for the MTV generation, who can't wait for their sporting gratification. I feel truly sorry for those sad souls that choose the instant, 20/20 fix over the splendour that is Test cricket; it must be like always having just a starter, when you could have had a three course meal. CS


20/20: Any innovation that makes this tedious, duffer's game shorter has to be applauded. WOL

# Question 38

# Nigella or Delia?

**NIGELLA:** I liked Nigella from the first time I saw her. She was beautiful and obviously intelligent. She was on one of those late-night book review programmes, which made me think I was one of the few people aware of her existence. What's more, her teeth looked slightly greyish-blue in the studio lighting, which made me hope that any other late-night saddos watching wouldn't find her as attractive as I did. I was in with a chance. A few years later, she hit the screens again as a hostess/chef extraordinaire. She looked gorgeous, her teeth were now white and she could cook, too! The media were all over her, so it was all over for me. Nevertheless, despite the growing fan base (and the growing Nigella), I have retained my fondness for her. She is the only person who could persuade me to eat sprouts – and make me want to boast about it to my friends afterwards.
Despite the terrible name and her overt sensuality, she is the kind of woman you would happily take home to meet your mum. Delia Smith, on the other hand, *is* your mum. **WOL**


**DELIA:** Delia isn't concerned with showing off her vast cookery skills; she just wants to help you hone yours. She's an unselfish cook – she says: "Look how I can help you!" not "Look at me!"
My mother-in-law gave each one of her sons Delia's *How to Cook* book when they left home and it's made men of them all. No man ever actually made one of Nigella's recipes, mainly because the pages tend to get stuck together.
Thanks to Delia, we can all boil an egg, clean our fingers without licking them and tell a cranberry from a redcurrant with ease. And I must say, she's never looked anything but minty-fresh to me. **FM**

# Question 39

# Duvet or sheets?

**DUVET:** Anyone who sleeps in sheets sleeps alone. They are constricting, uncomfortable and make sharing a bed nigh on impossible. Take it from this incessant fidget, a duvet is the only way to go. Only hospitals and foreign hotels still use sheets. Men who continue with the tradition of the sheet have a Peter Pan complex and won't leave their childhood behind. Women, if you spot a sheet in his bedroom, turn on your heel and run like the wind. Also, because a duvet allows the air to circulate, it doesn't provide a haven for bed bugs to mix, mingle and plan which part of you to eat first. **CS**


**SHEETS:** There's nothing like the cosy, comforting, safe feeling you get from slipping between freshly laundered sheets. It reminds me of when my mum would come and tuck me in before I went to sleep and I realise now that Scandinavians are probably the way they are – cold and distant – because they weren't tucked in at night by their mums. You can't tuck someone in with a duvet.

In adulthood, of course, my needs are different, but even now, sheets win hands-down. Firstly, a firmly tucked sheet-and-blanket combo is very difficult for a woman to pull over with her as she turns in her sleep (you can never sleep with a woman *and* a duvet, you can only ever end up with one of them).

Secondly, a duvet is no good in a fancy-dress party emergency. You always end up going as a marshmallow. With a sheet, you can be anything, from Julius Caesar to the ghost of Julius Caesar, in seconds. The simple, white sheet is a lifesaver; a sail if you're shipwrecked, a way to lower yourself out of a burning building, a parachute, and remember, if a hit man bursts into your room, he can't use a sheet to muffle the shots. **WOL**

# Question 40

# Shackleton or Scott?

**SHACKLETON:** Shackleton's leadership skills and courage are legendary. Scott might be hailed as the achiever, but Shackleton is the hero. He always put his men before himself and their lives even came before his own dreams of Antarctic glory. No one in Shackleton's party would have been allowed to "step outside" or be "some time". No, they would have been back in the tent and having a nip of brandy before you could say "frostbite". The names of their respective ships sum it all up: Shackleton's *Endurance* (steadfast, patient, tolerant, and simply bloody marvellous), as opposed to Scott's *Terra Nova* (obvious, boring and arrogant). **CS**


**SCOTT:** So Scott lost some men. Including himself. But at least he had some successful expeditions before the one he's famous for. Shackleton never got where he wanted to go, he just never hurt anyone while he was failing.

Scott is the ultimate - and yet typical - English gentleman explorer of his time; blind self-belief, self-sacrifice in the pursuit of glory, and complete dignity and sense of propriety in the face of total destruction. Scott passed the final test; he died like a gentleman. Only a real hero can suffer both failure and death and still emerge as an icon. **WOL**

# Question 41

# Great Fire or Great Plague?

**GREAT FIRE:** So much cleaner and don't forget the fantastic town planning opportunities. If it seems like a difficult Question, just ask yourself: Christopher Wren or bubos? That makes it much easier. Nobody likes a bubo. **FM**


**GREAT PLAGUE:** You really got your money's worth with the Great Plague. There were horrible physical symptoms, it attacked without warning, decimated communities, lasted for ages and destroyed people's faith in a benevolent God. The plague gave us red crosses on doors, plague pits and pustules - and a disaster isn't really a disaster without a pustule. The Great Fire just can't compete with this kind of heavyweight commitment to horror and destruction, so it should just give up and go out. **CS**

# Question 42

# Painting or sculpture?

**PAINTING:** A painting is a window into another world, a glimpse of another person's psyche, a journey into a different existence. Bizarrely, I find sculpture too one-dimensional; what you see is what you get and it leaves less room for the imagination to work its magic. Paint is a more versatile and more sophisticated medium. It involves creating an intriguing distance between the painting and the spectator, inviting your mind to work along with your senses to bridge that gap and allowing you greater possibilities for exploring your own reactions. Sculpture relies on a more primal, physical response, which is only half the story. **CS**


**SCULPTURE:** Sculpture is special. You can't pop into Athena and buy a Henry Moore. Nor is it likely that anybody will ever flog you a sculpture, then admit that a five-year-old made it, like art dealers love to do with paintings. Sculpture has so much more potential for interaction, too, even if you only buy one so you can cosh burglars with it.

I also think it's important to remember that two out of the Seven Wonders of the World were statues. No murals made the grade, I'm afraid.

But the argument is clinched for me by the public nature of sculpture. If I'm going to be immortalised, I don't want some scrappy oil painting of me, hanging forgotten in some musty gallery. No, I want a mammoth, monumental statue – like the ones Lenin and Stalin did so well – a hundred feet high, on a big hill, so people can get fabulous, panoramic views out of my eyeballs. **FM**

# Question 43

# London or Paris?

**LONDON:** It's bigger, seedier, louder, more threatening, more polluted, less attractive and less tasteful. The public transport is a joke, it's horrendously expensive and its most popular attraction is a wheel. But that's because London wears its present, as well as its past, on its sleeve. It's still fascinating to peer between the shiny, mirrored commercial buildings and see the odd reminder that London has been around since the primordial slime. All this makes London a more honest capital than Paris. Despite its faults, London still has many amazing attractions and this balance of old and new, good and bad, pride and shame, makes it a fair representation of England, past and present. I've lived in London and I loved it. Paris is fantastic for tourists, but it's just too clean, too self-consciously chic and too full of Parisians to convince us that it really represents the whole of France. **WOL**


**PARIS:** I've got nothing against London, I lived there for ten years, but "London or Paris?" is like asking "Margaret Rutherford or Catherine Deneuve?" They both have great qualities, but on the whole, you could spend longer gazing at Catherine.

Paris is the city of love, the city of light, the most beautiful city in the world. She's a glittering prize; a dazzling, knowing damsel who has been fought over a million times. And for the most part, grateful Parisians know how to look after her. When they toyed with the idea of skyscrapers, they built the Tour Montparnasse, took one look at it and thought, nah, that's naff, and never allowed another to spoil the centre of town. If only London's planners had cared so much.

Paris has better everything: food, architecture, transport, fashion, churches, shops, museums, emperors, I could go on. But most wonderful of all is being able to take two hours over a glorious, French lunch and not needing to feel the slightest bit guilty. **FM**

# Question 44

# The glass:
# half-full or half-empty?

**HALF-FULL:** Because it is. It just is. Go get a glass and half-fill it. Now look, it's half-full. How is it possible that you could be so negative and obtuse as to see it any other way? We both agree that there's stuff in there. It's palpably filling up half the glass. You can't argue that there's stuff in the glass, so for God's sake, try to concentrate on what you've got, rather than wasting time pointlessly obsessing about what you haven't. Why would you do that? Why? Why? **FM**


**HALF-EMPTY:** Right, I've got my half-glass of water and I'm having a good look, a really good look and…it's half-empty. It's clear to me that the whole top area of the vessel is completely vacant, unoccupied, without contents. There's not a vestige of a liquid anywhere to be found. A void. Not filled; ergo, empty. This is not about wanting what I haven't got; it's about my acceptance of the fact that the universe is an imperfect place. I'm just looking realistically at our flawed existence and not feeling the need to bestow upon it a glossy sheen of pointless optimism. **CS**

# Question 45

# Denim or corduroy?

**DENIM:** An invention more useful than fire, in my opinion. If the world wore corduroy, then the world would be celibate. Denim won the West; it's frontier material, cool and sexy. It conjures up images of handsome men on motorbikes wearing leather jackets, not red-complexioned, public schoolboys with bad teeth and braying laughs. Without jeans there wouldn't have been anything for rebellious youth to wear, there would be no Method acting and no need for the plunge bra. Well, what's the point in trying to pull a man in corduroy? **CS**


**CORDUROY:** Literally 'the cloth of kings', but it was also the trouser of choice for thousands of nineteenth century navvies, so it has a solid, working man's heritage as well. Corduroy's roots are genuinely more working-class than denim, but it also oozes quality, so it's acceptable in places where denim isn't. Denim supporters have tried to seek revenge for this by trying to convince the world that cord is only worn by Open University professors and geography teachers. That may be true, but these are intelligent people. George W. Bush wears denim.

The crowning glory of owning a pair of decent, down-to-earth cords is that no poncey fashion house would dare rip you off by putting a fancy label on them and charging you the earth. **WOL**

# Question 46

# Multiplex or arthouse?

**MULTIPLEX:** If an arthouse film is any good, you'll see it at a multiplex eventually. Then you can actually enjoy it; in comfier seats, with a bigger screen, bigger choice of snacks and much bigger portions. The ads are better, too. **WOL**


**ARTHOUSE:** You aren't expected to share the auditorium with people who think it's a restaurant, or who have failed to realise that talking loudly and inanely throughout a film can ruin it somewhat. An arthouse cinema usually isn't the size of Battersea power station, so you aren't forced to walk for days to find your chosen film; the adverts don't last longer than the feature and the carpets aren't designed to damage a retina. **CS**

# Question 47

# Spearmint or peppermint?

**SPEARMINT:** The mint of the connoisseur. Sweeter, gentler and more subtle, spearmint lulls the palate into paroxysms of tender delight. It's playful, yet at the same time delicate and refined. This is no wham-bam-blow-the-roof-of-yer-mouth-off-ma'am, peppermint assault. Eschew those coarse excesses. Surrender to the sophisticated caress of the spear and softly embrace the deeper mysteries of mint. **FM**


**PEPPERMINT:** There is clearly no point to spearmint whatsoever. It has no flavour at all. I've checked. Peppermint makes your mouth feel glacier fresh, mountain stream-like and ready for anything. Spearmint just pretends it might and then refuses, point blank. Where mint is concerned, subtlety can take a hike. My taste buds like to be taken hard, fast and up against a wall; they don't like to be prodded about by an amateur. **CS**

# Question 48

# Testaments: Old or New?

**OLD:** It's bold, it's brassy, it's enormous. We get hellfire, damnation, parting seas, dreams, plagues, not to mention flaming bushes; indeed, the whole kit and caboodle. And if that gets you rather overexcited, then read the Psalms, or the Song of Solomon – some of the most beautiful poetry ever written. If anyone professes to prefer the New to the Old, they're clearly demonstrating a complete lack of balls and imagination. Loving your neighbour isn't nearly so much fun as smiting their ox. **CS**


**NEW:** In the case of the Bible, 'new' really does mean improved. The Old Testament God is jealous and vengeful, always smiting stuff and demanding sacrifices. And the plot! "…And Enos begat Am-a-lek…and Am-a-lek begat Ma-hal-a-leel…and Ma-hal-a-leel begat Na-hath…and Na-hath lived eight hundred and forty years…" And this is just the first book, after which there are another thirty-eight to go until you get the New Testament.

Thankfully, the New presents us with a new God, who loves us, never mentions ram slaughtering and makes everything nicely psychedelic. The New Testament has it all - part biography, part epic, part sci-fi - but it really plays its ace at the end, with Revelations. If you only ever read one book of the whole Bible, make it Revelations. There are dragons, a woman riding a seven-headed beast with ten horns, locusts the size of horses with "teeth as the teeth of Lions", and many more, all competing in the final battle between Good and Evil, before the world ends.

J.R.R. Tolkien has nothing on this stuff. **WOL**

# Question 49

# Hitler or Stalin?

**HITLER:** The old "Evil or evil?" Question is always difficult. It demands deep consideration, but basically, I think the best thing you can say about Hitler is that without him, we'd never have had *The Producers*; a creation so sublime, it almost makes the Second World War worthwhile. Nor, as far as Britain is concerned, would we have had *Dad's Army*, *'Allo 'Allo*, or even *It Ain't Half Hot, Mum*. All you get with Stalin is *The Gulag Archipelago* and there's no material for Jimmy Perry and David Croft in that. **FM**


**STALIN:** It all comes down to a question of hair. Stalin had better hair, both on his head and on his upper lip. The word that springs to mind is 'luxuriant'. In fact, I'm prepared to assert that he had the best hair of any genocidal dictator in history. **CS**

# Question 50

# Chocolate: milk or dark?

**MILK:** I don't want to be grown-up. I just want nice, creamy, gentle chocolate that makes me happy. Dark chocolate is bitter and twisted and ruins otherwise lovely things like Black Magic.
When I was a kid, the Cadbury's advert showed someone breaking a bar of Dairy Milk and o, miracle! Out poured a glass and a half of full-cream milk. Images like that stay with you. It was so brilliant; I used to carefully snap my new bars in two, hoping the milk would come out. It never did, but it was a wonderful dream to have.
Dark chocolate makes my head hurt. **FM**


**DARK:** There is no excuse for those sad souls, those friends of Satan, who have (entirely voluntarily, mind) selected the heinous crime that is milk chocolate. Why would you pick that tasteless mass of chemicals and sugar, that's barely brushed passed a cocoa bean, when you can experience the intense, gastronomic explosion of the real thing? Milk chocolate eaters aren't eating chocolate at all, but something concocted in a physics lab. They should all be rounded up and imprisoned for imposing wanton, masochistic cruelty on their taste buds. Imprisoned, I say! **CS**

# Question 51

# Breakfast: Full English or continental?

**FULL ENGLISH:** With both breakfast options, you'll get some orange juice, a choice of tea or coffee, and a pot of jam or marmalade (with the Full English, the latter comes with the rack of toast that invariably arrives before the main plate). So, ultimately, the choice is between a flimsy pastry on one hand, or a plate of sausages, bacon, mushrooms, tomato, fried toast, beans and hash browns on the other. Black pudding is another option, as is haggis in the Full Scottish.

What's the sense in going for the continental? You've paid for the breakfast anyway, you would never make a Full English breakfast for yourself at home, and you can fill up now and save money by not having to buy lunch. (If you feel peckish later, you could maybe buy a croissant to see you through to dinner.) **WOL**


**CONTINENTAL:** Did you get up at 3am, go lambing, plough a few fields, then milk the herd? No? So what makes you think you're entitled to a Full English breakfast? Unless you're a proper, labouring man, eating that much saturated fat first thing in the morning simply proves that you're yet another bloated consumer who should know better.

The continental, with its obligatory and divine croissants, is the new breakfast of civilisation. Even when you're eating it in grey, rainy Britain, you can close your eyes, dip your pastry in your coffee, and pretend you're in a Parisian pavement café. **FM**

# Question 52

# Hurricane or Spitfire?

**HURRICANE:** The first woman I meet who can answer this question becomes Mrs O'Leary. I champion the Hurricane because it's perennially underrated. It won the Battle of Britain, but the Spitfire always muscles in on the credit. There were more Hurricanes – 32 squadrons to the Spitfire's 19 – and they made more kills. A Hurricane shot down the first Luftwaffe plane of the war. It was slower and heavier, but it was steadier and safer. Get hit in a Hurricane and at least you had a fighting chance. It's the real survivor; the workhorse, not the racehorse. It's the one that got the job done. **WOL**


**SPITFIRE:** Thanks for the proposal, sweetie, but I'll have to say no. Nor will I indulge in a dogfight with the beloved Hurricane. All I can say is – give me glamour. Call me superficial, but I'm under the Spitfire's spell. Everything you say is true, but the Spitfire was much faster, had better manoeuvrability, better range and - despite the increased risk - given the choice, I'd rather have flown a Spitfire than a Hurricane. And so would the Luftwaffe. It was the only plane that could outfly the Messerschmitt 109 and when Goering asked one German ace what he needed to ensure victory in the Battle of Britain, the pilot replied: "A squadron of Spitfires". **FM**

# Question 53

# Boots or Superdrug?

**BOOTS:** Boots cares. **CS**


**SUPERDRUG:** Superdrug's cheaper. (Allegedly.) **FM**

# Question 54

# Diarrhoea or vomit?

**DIARRHOEA:** I have never accidentally trodden in diarrhoea while walking back from the pub on a Saturday night. Nor have I ever felt moved towards sympathetic diarrhoea when hearing someone else have an attack of the trots. Likewise, being at sea in a storm has never loosed my bowels. Bowels are more reliable than stomachs. People are constantly vomiting in public, but I have yet to see someone's trousers explode. For that reason alone, diarrhoea wins for me. **WOL**


**VOMIT:** You know where you are with sick. It's precisely because people throw up all the time that it's not scary. You know exactly where it came from and why. I *have* seen someone's trousers explode - it wasn't pretty and it's not an experience I'm planning to repeat any time soon. It's against the natural order of the universe for anything related to the bowels to be witnessed. I can't deal with the brown stuff in any way - it comes from the darkest recesses of the body and should stay there. For the love of God, give me something that comes out resembling (if only vaguely) what it was when it went in. Give me something I can relate to, know how to clear up and can spell. **CS**

# Question 55

# Evolution or Creation?

**EVOLUTION:** Evolution is our past – it is what has happened to us. Yet it's also what *is* happening, and will continue to happen, to us. It's the more dynamic choice; it is about process, development, becoming and change. Creation is an event; a static, isolated happening. Evolution also connects us with nature; it reminds us where we came from and that we're a part of the bigger picture. I don't know why the bible-bashers hate Darwin so much. He didn't deny the existence of God (though his work was used by others to do so), but he did put the ball in our court and reminded us that we can't blame everything on God. Evolution also explains why, whenever I see a chimpanzee, I think of my brother.

More importantly, without the Theory of Evolution, *Planet of the Apes* wouldn't make any sense at all. **WOL**


**CREATION:** I see this one as more of a social tool for single women, rather than a deeply held belief. You can have so much fun with it, trust me. The instructions are simple: select the man of your choice, ply him with a couple of drinks, ensure an ample amount of cleavage is on display, ask this Question and declare for Creation. He'll be there for hours, telling you how wrong you are and how right he is. After a while, mention that while his superlative defence of Evolution has convinced you that Darwin was probably right, think how much fun it would be to discuss what you'd do with a free week and unlimited powers. No doubt, he'll tell you exactly what he'd do. You nod, you stare deeply into his eyes and then, when he's finished and the pub is closed, you take him home and you show him that there is a God. **CS**

# Question 56

# Call or email?

**CALL:** It's a dark and stormy night. A flash of lightning illuminates the street and you catch a fleeting glimpse of the escaped killer you've just seen on the news. He's across the road, just about to break into that house where Jennifer Love Hewitt is all alone. What do you do? Turn the computer on and wait five minutes to start up, log on, then send her an email saying "Get out of the house, now"?

Of course, email has its place, but generally speaking, it's a cold and impersonal form of human communication that places a deliberate distance between two people. An email says "I don't really want to waste my time talking to you, so I'll just spend a few minutes typing something out - seeing as I'm on the computer anyway". A phone call says "I'd like to be with you, but distance or time doesn't permit. This is the next best thing". It's also the most effective way of saying "I care about you enough to alert you to the fact that there's a killer in your living room". **WOL**


**EMAIL:** It doesn't have to be cold and impersonal. Emails can be chatty and amusing, and when they are, you can print them out and keep them forever.

But OK, I admit it, they're often an excuse not to talk to somebody, and you know what? Sometimes, I would rather disembowel myself with a soup spoon than talk to somebody. What will I say to them? What will they say to me? What mad, unexpected, cringemaking pap will I come out with? Will my mouth and brain hook up? Will there be uncontrollable jabbering? Anything could happen.

An email gives me control. I can say what I mean, without being interrupted, disagreed with, or resembling Stanley Unwin after dental surgery. That's all I ask – to express myself properly. And in a way that will always stand up in court. **FM**

# Question 57

# Manet or Monet?

**MANET:** Manet's the one for me. I love his work on both an aesthetic and a political level. He was brave enough to hold a mirror up to the hypocritical, Parisian middle classes and they didn't like what they saw one bit. He was also courageous in challenging his audience's attitudes to women and sex, using the very medium that was supposed to reassure and please them. Manet doesn't paint mythological or literary characters, but women who sold sex to men rich enough to be able to afford it. These same men were often the ones standing in the gallery, staring at the women on canvas – and Manet's women stared right back. But it's not just his politics or subject matter that make me catch my breath. Manet dispensed with the usual niceties in art; he used simple design, limited palette and bold brush strokes. Unlike Monet, he dealt with people. He couldn't divorce himself from the society in which he lived, to concentrate on an abstract idea. He was a modern painter with a modern technique, but his work is more than mere theory made manifest and that's the way I like it. **CS**


**MONET:** Impressionism isn't so much a school of art as a right of passage. It's a period you go through when you first get to university, college, or even just adulthood, and feel the need to show how smart and sophisticated you are. A quick trip to Athena would furnish you with some cheap facsimile of something that matched your idea of 'cultured' and it would usually be a Monet. The water lilies, the girl with a brolly on a hill, the women (with brollies and bonnets) in a field of poppies…at least fifty per cent of student accommodation would have one of these Blu-tacked to the wall.
Most people grow out of Impressionism by the time they're twenty-one, but for that brief period when you needed to find a way of showing that, despite all appearances, you had actually discovered and embraced 'culture', Monet was there to help you prove it. **WOL**

# Question 58

# Too hot or too cold?

**TOO HOT:** To be honest, I can't really see how anybody could be too hot, except perhaps Joan of Arc. Hot is lovely. If I'm going to die of an extreme temperature, please let it be hot. Cold is a nightmare; it's the retreat from Moscow, the Gulags, the house of your friend who never has the heating on and opens the windows in January. It's hell.

Why do we go to hot places in summer, when it's already hot here? Because people can't be too warm. Heat is any mammal's natural preference. Think of it this way – Iceland or Italy? Italy, obviously, although to be fair, Iceland does have those hot springs and offers a chance to wear lots of lovely, fleecy clothing.

We talk about hot dates, hot legs, hot pants and hot dogs - these are all good things. Hot is good. It's never really too hot, but if you honestly feel it is, just slip into the pool. **FM**


**TOO COLD:** I always feel that life is teasing me when it gets too hot. The higher the temperature, the fewer clothes women wear. On really hot days, the parks and beaches can be as good as any erotic nightclub - and no one is charging you £50 for a drink. The problem is that I'm there, sapped of all energy, with my clothes drenched in sweat, looking and feeling like I've just completed a double marathon. None of the under-clad women would want to take me home, even if I had the energy to do something.

Being too cold means snuggling up in front of the fire, drinking lots of whisky or brandy, then retiring to bed. She'll say, "Ooh, it's so cold, how on earth do we keep ourselves warm?" Well, I have an idea…**WOL**

# Question 59

# Film star or rock star?

**FILM STAR:** It's the best form of immortality. Even Elvis thought so, or he wouldn't have risked his reputation as a rock-god in order to achieve screen cred.

Film stars are invited to better parties, look more glamorous and people pay more attention to them. Screen stardom has real cachet. Can you remember any Grammy winners from last year? Probably not, but I bet you know who was Best Actor at the Oscars.

Being a film star is also much easier than being a rock star. You could even play a rock star in a film, try out the lifestyle and be paid millions for it, without the grind of performing in sweat-drenched stadiums and muddy fields every night for years on end, trying desperately to reprise your youth by wearing ludicrous clothes and catching unmentionable diseases from drug-addled groupies.

Nicole Kidman or Courtney Love? Sean Connery or Rod Stewart? Hooray for Hollywood. **FM**


**ROCK STAR:** If you are a creative soul looking for a career, consider that the music route allows you to express yourself in your own words and own way, whereas acting only allows you to interpret what someone else wants you to say, or do.

But I am not a creative soul and, for me, this Question is really a simple choice between a life swishing about at la-di-da parties, drinking champagne and eating canapés with all the la-di-da darlings, or  rolling around in expensive hotel suites with an orgy of teenage girls, drunk as a lord and high on coke. (Try doing this as an actor and it'll be a scandal, but for a rock star it's required behaviour.)

Also, I can't help noticing that if you start off with a career in music, there's a good chance you can go on to become a film star – Frank Sinatra, Dean Martin, Barbara Streisand, Will Smith – but it's a lot more difficult the other way around. Think William Shatner, Russell Crowe, Keanu Reeves… Need I go on? **WOL**

# Question 60

# Cowboy or Indian?

**COWBOY:** They won, all right? I'm genuinely deeply sorry about what happened to the Native Americans, and the bison, but the cowboys had better outfits, much better films and they won.

I had a cowgirl costume when I was little. I was a sheriff and I had a fantastic, silver gun with a red handle that I fought my cousin Darren for. It was no contest. I loved that gun. Why would I want to be an Indian when I had silver guns and silver badges, a fabulous, big hat and an attractively fringed skirt? Bang! Bang! I won the West! **FM**


**INDIAN:** Most importantly, the Native Americans had the moral right on their side. They were incredible horsemen (that's horse–*men*) and didn't need to fart about with girly stuff, like saddles and chaps, unlike the cowboys (cow–*boys*). The Indians might not have had guns, but they did scalp their enemies. How cool is that? Hack that stupid settler's hairpiece off, that's what I say.

They also had better names - Sitting Bull and Running Water knock the spots off anything the cowboys could come up with. They had far more versatile hair, a more tasteful wardrobe and didn't eat beans. **CS**

# Question 61

# Astronomy or astrology?

**ASTRONOMY:** The Earth sits in a nice little gathering of nine planets, clustered around the sun. The sun is our closest star. The Sun is one of approximately 200,000,000,000 stars that make up our galaxy, the Milky Way. Our galaxy is one of about 100 billion floating around in the universe. The universe is very big. There are trillions of planets, and it takes about 18 billion years for the light from our sun to reach the furthest stars in the universe.

On a really dark night, you can see somewhere between 1000 and 1500 stars with the naked eye. Do you really think that our nine planets and these particular stars are specifically trying to tell you that your lucky colour is orange, or that the month of August will have a surprise in store for you? Get a life, you moron. **WOL**


**ASTROLOGY:** There are more things in heaven and earth, William, than you appear to be able to tolerate. I'm with Jung on this one, especially since he pointed out that modern astrology has developed directly from the ancient world's vast, but underrated, psychological knowledge. The star signs are celestial archetypes. Spot on, Carl.

We're all part of the same universe and made of the same stuff. All astrology tries to do is explain this in terms of psychology, rather than physics. By all means, ignore the Mystic Megs of this world and let's hear it for the Hubble telescope, but keep your mind open. Think about the tides. Vast oceans are pushed and pulled by a bit of rock 239,000 miles away. Given that the moon can do that, do you really think you're so big and so clever that it couldn't possibly influence you? **FM**

# Question 62

# Assassinating JFK: lone gunman or conspiracy?

**LONE GUNMAN:** Why not just ask: "Lone gunman or little green men?" For anybody who doesn't understand that Oliver Stone made a movie and not a documentary, let me put it plainly. World leaders get shot. It happens quite regularly. It happened to Spencer Perceval, but people didn't freak out that big lizards from Outer Space were to blame.

Oswald had attempted an assassination before. He was a good shot. He was photographed with a gun and holding a newspaper, to show the date. He fired the gun from his place of work and killed Kennedy. The bullet wasn't magic – it went through people just like you'd expect. Is this scenario disappointingly ordinary for you? Would you like more lizards, perhaps dressed as FBI operatives?

OK, here's the truth: Elvis did it, with Paul McCartney – but not the one we've got now, the one who died in 1966 and was replaced with a clone. They were put up to it by the baby-eating Illuminati who control the world. If you play back Princess Di's last interview in slow motion and reverse the tape, you can clearly hear her saying: "Elvis killed Kennedy and if you don't believe me, you're off your grassy knoll". **FM**


**CONSPIRACY:** Even if Lee Harvey Oswald was the only gunman firing at JKF that day, it doesn't prove that there was no conspiracy.

I first became suspicious when looking at a website called The Kennedy Assassination, which promised "constantly updated and truthful information". When I clicked on it, the "this page cannot be displayed" notice appeared. Hmm.

Also, have you noticed that the word 'conspiracy' is itself an anagram of 'CIA Corn Spy' and that corn is grown in Louisiana – the very state in which Oswald was born?

Corn also provides a bizarre and unexplored link with Margaret Thatcher. JFK was assassinated on 22 November 1963, the same date on which Mrs Thatcher resigned as Prime Minister, a mere 27 years later. She was leader of the Conservatives, the very same Party that repealed the Corn Laws in 1846 – the same year Abraham Lincoln was elected to Congress!

Your deprecation of the conspiracy theory only leads me to suspect that you yourself are either a CIA operative, one of the lizard-people, or a Tory. **WOL**

# Question 63

# Porsche or Ferrari?

**PORSCHE:** There is a long answer, but basically a Porsche is far more reliable than a Ferrari. It's Teutonic efficiency versus mad, noisy Italian chaos. Or - as I prefer to think of it - cool, curvy German frauleins versus tempestuous, high-maintenance Latin signorinas. The no-nonsense girls will get you there in style, while the prima donnas are throwing hissy fits on the hard shoulder at midnight. **WOL**


**FERRARI:** God, who cares about bleeding efficiency? If I'm going to ride in a pointlessly expensive, totally impractical phallic symbol, I don't want to mess around. I want it big, I want it red and I want it to have an engine that could fire rockets to the moon. I want to sit two inches from the tarmac, in seats covered with the hind of some hapless animal, in front of a dashboard resembling a cockpit. To hell with practicality, to hell with mechanical precision, I want to make a statement and I want to make it in something wild, extrovert and Italian. **CS**

# Question 64

# M&S or BHS?

**MARKS AND SPENCER:** In M&S, I am able foster the illusion that I'm a hip chick about town. It's so reassuringly expensive and so well carpeted. It sells sexy lingerie and pre-chopped leeks (because, sweetie, life's just too short to slice!). It gives me specially designed bags during the Christmas season and fantastic air conditioning in the summer. British Home Stores does none of those things; it's dark, chaotic and the underbelly of retail therapy. It's the home of those that have given up on the dream of a better shopping life. **CS**


**BHS:** You're so wrong. BHS is bright, light, welcoming, unpretentious and, unlike M&S, there's no messing about in different sections, with different labels, at all sorts of different - usually rather high - prices. As far as I can see, you can buy more or less the same stuff, only much, much cheaper. (Allegedly.) **FM**

# Question 65

# Microsoft or Mac?

**MICROSOFT:** I'm not a designer. I don't waft around sleek offices, with nothing in them but a vase of tulips, creating divine concepts on my state-of-the-zeitgeist computer. I just want it to help me type. Microsoft may be the ubiquitous bane of people's lives, it may be the epitome of vile consumerism, it may even cause cancer, but it works for me. I don't know any other way and I'm not interested in finding out.

Think of Microsoft as the new English language. People may despise it, people may not want to use it, but most of the world does. We all know how it works and it gets the job done. Mac is the Gaelic language. In comparison, hardly anybody understands it, but those that do think they're really, really great. **FM**


**MAC:** If Microsoft were a woman, you'd dump her.

It's annoying that she can be so slow and so illogical, because you know she's actually quite bright and has the capacity to do so much more than she will ever let on. This is made worse by the fact that you know she really makes an effort at work, in the office, but is deliberately more contrary at home. Things are going along just fine when, all of a sudden, she gets annoyed for no apparent reason and throws you out. "What did I do wrong?" you ask – but she won't tell.

On the other hand, Mac is really lovely. She's open and easy-going, yet intelligent and sophisticated. OK, so she tends to hang around with artists and professional types, but if you make the effort to approach her, you'll find that she's not deliberately discriminating; it's just that her penchant for the well-turned-out designer look makes most people assume she's too high maintenance for them. They're wrong. I'm moving in with Mac, especially since I realised how many other men were playing with Microsoft's X-Box. **WOL**

# Question 66

# Host or guest?

**HOST:** I'll cook, I'll clean, I'll pretty much do anything to avoid the burden that being a guest carries. I can't bear the worry of being in someone else's house, not knowing where everything is and how everything works. What if I'm too cold, or too hot? What if they all get up at five in the morning? What happens if I'm served something horrific at supper, which is impossible to force down with a smile? What happens if I'm taken ill during the night, because of the horrific something I've eaten earlier, and the bathroom is a three day trek from my bedroom? What if the sheets are dirty and the bed resembles a mediaeval torture instrument? What happens if I'm not given enough alcohol? Call me a control freak, call me what you like, but don't call and ask me to stay. **CS**


**GUEST:** It's great. You go to someone's house, they do everything for you. What's not to like? All you have to do is be polite and be prepared to indulge any peculiarities your host may have. Once you accept that, it's like being in a hotel and not paying. There's no cleaning – before or after  and no cooking. In fact, there's none of the nasty stuff, just good food and good company. Only peasants hate being guests, because they can't cope with being waited on. Relax, surrender to the glorious symbiosis of the situation, and have a glass of the wine you brought as a present. All my friends are hosts. **FM**

# Question 67

# Crisps: salt 'n' vinegar or cheese 'n' onion?

**SALT 'N' VINEGAR:** It's a real, organic flavour. There's salt and there's vinegar – it's a divine, naturally occurring taste experience. The combination is punchy and piquant, yet it doesn't overpower the potato, so a salt 'n' vinegar crisp is a perfectly balanced crisp.

Cheese 'n' onion doesn't just taste filthy; it's synthetic flavouring at its worst. Nobody would actively seek out the combination of cheese and onion in everyday life. Things would have to come to a very pretty pass indeed for anyone normal to crave such an abomination. So who on earth would want a crisp to taste like that?

There are some things in life everybody should be able to rely on, and one of them is that salt 'n' vinegar crisps come in blue packets and cheese 'n' onion come in green ones. For the safety of salt 'n' vinegar lovers, the observation of this convention is vital. When a certain crisp manufacturer - whom I no longer patronise - swapped the colours around in the Nineties, I accidentally bought the wrong pack and nearly had a seizure. **FM**


**CHEESE 'N' ONION:** There are some things that are meant to be, that are written in the stars and on the wind. The meeting and melding of cheese with onion is one such occurrence. The cheese is Romeo to the onion's Juliet; they may come from different families, but their fate is entwined and they are meant to be forever united in a crisp packet. There is nothing organic about vinegar, nothing at all. It's used to clean kettles, for God's sake. I don't enjoy having the roof of my mouth taken off, which is why I hate salt 'n' vinegar crisps. Where's the sense in drowning perfectly good potatoes in vast amounts of salt and acid? Where, please? **CS**

# Question 68

# Boy/Girl Scouts or Boys'/Girls' Brigade?

**SCOUTS:** I always thought "Never the twain shall meet" until I found out Baden-Powell got the idea for the Scouts after the founder of the Boys' Brigade asked him to write an article for their newsletter. Nowadays, though, if you're a member of one organisation, chances are that the other is a complete mystery to you.

I was a Brownie dropout; a renegade Elf. I had quite enjoyed it, but nurtured ambitions to move up from seconder to sixer, the top job, which I felt had my name on it. The attempted *coup d'etat* not only went horribly wrong, it coincided with getting my Jester's badge, which was way too much serendipity to bear.

I have to champion Scouting because it's all I know. There were some Boys' Brigade kids in my street, but they looked like Thunderbirds and never talked to anyone. My cousin was a Queen's Guide, so I suppose I might be in line for some sort of royal pardon for my transgressions, but I know for sure that the other Elves will never forgive me. **FM**


**BRIGADE:** I joined the Cubs with my friend Jason, mainly for the uniform. Soon after, I saw a lad walking through town in a smart blue uniform and white gloves. I had never heard of the Boys' Brigade until then, but I became fascinated by the fact that there was a rival organization to the Scouts. Although the different uniforms made me imagine we were Che Guevara's band of revolutionaries and the Brigade were the Bolivian Army, the expected conflict between the two groups never materialized, nor was it encouraged. Why? The reason became all too obvious - *both* organizations were just a tool of bourgeois conformists, a training ground for drones of the capitalist workplace and military machine.

Thanks to the Boys' Brigade, my eyes were opened to the awful truth and I got the seed of an idea that led me and Comrade Jason to form the first UK branch of the Young Komsomols. We became the mortal enemies of the bourgeois Scouts, though they never knew it. **WOL**

# Question 69

# At the cinema: front row or back row?

**FRONT ROW:** I'm here to see the film and the front row is the best place to see it – certainly no further back than row F, anyway. Ensconced at the front, I'm not disturbed by the zombies who wander out to the loo during crucial scenes, or the bobbing heads of cretinous teenagers. I am mistress of all I survey.

The front row is for those of us who paid to see the film and want our money's worth. This position gives maximum concentration potential. The fidgeting, fussing, faffing and fiddling are all behind you. You can block them out entirely. The reprobates on the back row are only there because they can't afford a room, but I'm on the front row because the one-to-one relationship I want is with the actors on screen and nobody, but nobody, is going to come between us. **FM**


**BACK ROW:** What was it I saw, the first time I went to the cinema with a girl? Lucy Ramsden's bra! What film was showing? Who cares? I saw Lucy Ramsden's bra. I had a go at undoing it as well, quickly and badly, before giving up because she stopped kissing me and looked at me in that way that says "What the hell do you think you're doing?" As I had absolutely no idea, we resumed our canoodling. Ah, the back row! Refuge for ardent youth.

Now I'm older and no longer know where Lucy Ramsden is, I sit in the middle row and actually watch the film. My cinema-going experience has not been enhanced as a result. **WOL**

# Question 70

# Jam or marmalade?

**JAM:** I'm very delicate first thing in the morning and my system can't take any sudden shocks. Putting lumps of shredded citrus in my mouth at an early hour is more than I can bear. I need to be lulled from my bed, with the gentle, fruity sweetness of jam.

Jam will never hurt me. Jam won't give my taste buds shock therapy before I've fully opened my eyes. Jam is my friend and stays with me throughout the day, greeting me from the centre of my Jammie Dodger and beneath the cream on my teatime scone. Not even marmalade devotees want to see that vicious condiment hanging around after breakfast time. It thinks it's hard, but it's really just a bully. If I wanted to be woken with that much of a jolt, I'd stick my tongue in the toaster. **FM**


**MARMALADE:** My dad always told me it puts hairs on your chest and increases your sperm count (thick-cut variety only). It's jam, for men. **WOL**

# Question 71

# Books: fold the corner or use a bookmark?

**CORNER FOLD:** For me, bookmarks are useless frippery and fall into the same category as silver-plated tie clips, serviette holders and engraved platinum toothpicks. I have a fairly utilitarian approach to books. Don't get me wrong - I love them. I have hundreds of them, because I've always hoped that any woman visiting my pad will be impressed by the sheer number of books I own and the awesome breadth of subjects with which I am conversant. Having a lot of books says "I'm bright and I'm getting even brighter". There are many men out there who buy books for this very reason – to give the impression of learnedness. Folding the page corner gives me the edge over most of these pretenders, because it looks as though my books have actually been read. **WOL**


**BOOKMARK:** My God, you filthy barbarian. You're the sort of person who draws on maps, aren't you? I think I need to lie down.
To tamper with a book in any way is pure Philistinism. Books are to be treasured. By all means, read them until the spines are broken and the covers frayed, but don't ever do deliberate, wilful damage. A bookmark can be anything – a postcard, an old lottery ticket, an unwanted skin-graft. You don't *have* to buy it from a National Trust shop. The important thing is that it can be lifted out as if it had never been there. It's the ecological approach to reading – tread lightly and leave things as you found them. Future generations will thank you. **FM**

# Question 72

# Raincoat or umbrella?

**RAINCOAT:** I remember it clearly - September 11, 1978. A Bulgarian dissident, Georgi Markov, died after being poked in the leg with a poisoned umbrella. Ever since then, I've been acutely cautious around people with umbrellas. Although, generally speaking, I'm fairly certain that no one is actually out to kill me, I've observed that most people wield their brollies like crazed assassins. They seem intent on spearing my eyeball with one of the spokes, or forcing me into the path of an oncoming bus, because they take up all the pavement space with their bloody contraptions.

Umbrella people are either selfish bastards, or cold-hearted killers. OK, so perhaps the shifty man in the mac is the one who really intends to assassinate you, but at least there's no chance that you'll be accidentally killed or injured by his raincoat. **WOL**


**UMBRELLA:** Simple logistics. Keep the rain as far away from you as possible. Head it off at the pass with your umbrella, rather than letting it soak you and then having to wander around like a wet dog.

When the rain is over, an umbrella folds away invisibly to leave you pristine, whereas anybody in a raincoat remains wet for ages after a downpour. What's worse - sitting next to someone whose umbrella is dripping neatly in a nearby stand, or being stuck beside a drenched, steaming cagoule-wearer, with a bad case of catarrh?

As all women know, with an umbrella - or may I suggest a delightful parasol? - you're not stuck wearing a coat all day. You can dress how you like and still stay dry. **FM**

# Question 73

# Hamburger or fish and chips?

**HAMBURGER:** Despite all the many wondrous things that can be said in favour of fish and chips, and the numerous criticisms that can be levelled against fast-food hamburgers, probably the best things I ever tasted were my mum's home-made burgers (September 1981-July 1986). They were also the only meal she ever cooked successfully, because she wasn't trying to follow a Delia Smith recipe. These were her own invention. Well done, Mum. **WOL**


**FISH AND CHIPS:** Let me help you understand. You get chips – warm, wonderful, golden sticks of salty, fried heaven – and you also get fish. It's the perfect, can't-be-bothered-cooking-tonight meal and, being a proper meal, it scores even more points over the hamburger, which is traditionally eaten with one hand, while the other texts a drug dealer.
Fish and chips are a much-loved, Great British institution. They taste great and there's never any possibility you'll bite into a chip and pull out a lump of partially recovered testicle. There's also the warm feeling you get from knowing that no area of rainforest the size of Belgium was slashed and burned so you could dine in style. **FM**

# Question 74

# Greeks or Trojans?

**GREEKS:** Why would anyone vote Trojan? They were a ridiculous group of people.  Firstly, they insisted on fighting a gratuitous war with the far mightier Greeks, because Paris (a classical lounge lizard if ever there was one) had got bored with the nymph he was chasing and decided to pursue Helen instead. He put the lives of his fellow countrymen on the line in order to get his end away and they allowed him to do it.
Secondly, they invited a huge wooden horse into the city, despite being categorically told not to (by the gods, no less), which allowed the far superior Greeks to kick their ass. Something that I believe they richly deserved. **CS**


**TROJANS:** Forget that Aphrodite had officially promised Helen to Paris and that Helen never complained. Forget that even some Greeks thought it was a stupid war, like the King of Paphos, who offered fifty ships – one real and forty-nine toys. Forget that the Greeks were so dumb they couldn't find Troy at all at the first attempt, landed somewhere quite different and upset the natives there. Forget the arrogance and brutality of Agamemnon and Menelaus. Forget that Achilles liked a bit of cross-dressing. The reason to love Troy is Hector. Hector was a true champion – his mummy wasn't a goddess who got him special armour from Mount Olympus in case he hurt his little pinkie. He was just a man, but the bravest, soundest, most intelligent of men and he lost only because, unlike Achilles, he didn't have a ton of divine intervention. He was the only real, unblemished hero of the *Iliad*. In fact, Hector's my perfect man and I'd pop round his house any day. **FM**

# Question 75

# Physics or biology?

**PHYSICS:** At school, this was the hard science, the one with difficult maths. Biology was the easy science, the nice science, with pretty flowers and babies and animals. It was the girls' science.

Physics is about how the stuff we can't see makes the things we can see happen. It all started when Aristotle saw dust, floating about in the light streaming through his window, and thought "Gosh, those little bits of stuff must be what everything is made of". He was wrong, but also right. Now we know that the things everything is made of are themselves made of even smaller things. And we owe it to ourselves to take a look.

It scares people when we start splitting the atom. They associate this with war, and Weapons of Mass Destruction, and see physics as the antithesis of biology and its lovely plants and fluffy animals. People think that physics is the science of war and biology is the science of love. But they are wrong. Biology has become the science of war. Biology will kill us all. **WOL**


**BIOLOGY:** It might be the science that deals with animals, flowers and reproduction, but this makes biology far more relevant to everyday life than physics. Who cares about small floating particles? That's dust; buy a duster and it won't worry you any more. And splitting the atom just made a small thing smaller. Like cutting a pea in half, but noisier. Biology deals with the important stuff, like what goes where when you finally get the man, or woman, of your dreams into a compromising position.

At my school, biology explained where cheek cells go to die and we were invited to experience such unforgettable operations as squeezing a (dead) sheep's lungs and picking bits off half a pig's head. Physics merely involved crocodile clips and teachers with dandruff; an indication that this was a science for the lonely and socially inept. **CS**

# Question 76

# Tate Britain or Tate Modern?

**TATE BRITAIN:** Tate Britain presents the history of British art (from 1500 A.D. to the present) all under one roof. If, like me, you recoil at the thought of being confronted with an unwashed pair of Tracey Emin's knickers and you feel that the term 'BritArt' should really include the likes of Hogarth, Constable, Turner, Blake, Alma-Tadema, Waterhouse, Bacon and Hockney, then Tate Britain is for you. If, on the other hand, you have no idea at all about art, then it's still a great place to start. You won't like everything, but you're bound to see something you recognise from the last time you were trying to choose a suitable birthday card for your mum.

But if you think art is a room with a flickering light bulb, an unmade bed, a crumpled piece of paper, or a small amount of Blu-tack pressed to the wall, then by all means, go to the Tate Modern. Or just pop into a student bedsit. **WOL**


**TATE MODERN:** "It's just a pile of bricks." "It's an unmade bed." "My dog could do better." The same criticisms have been levelled at modern art since the term was coined. Of course, those who tend to go on and on about how they, too, could have cut up a cow and stuck it in formaldehyde, have never done so – nor, indeed, have they done anything remotely artistic, even during double art. There needs to be a place for the rebellious and experimental; before it becomes safe and acceptable. There needs to be a building able to cope with the possibility that art history could be made within its walls and the Tate Modern is one such building. It's bold, it's beautiful and it's huge. Where else could Olafur Eliasson's *The Weather Project* or Max Beckmann's works be shown to such powerful advantage? The Tate Modern is where I go to see modern art faultlessly exhibited; it's where I go when I want to remind myself why I live in London. **CS**

# Question 77

# Popcorn: salt or sweet?

**SALT:** Savoury popcorn is delicious, hugely moreish and a pleasure to masticate.

Selling sweet popcorn should be considered a criminal offence. The sugar metamorphoses an otherwise tasty snack into something that tastes like radioactive waste. I wouldn't feed it to my worst enemy. It's disgusting, against the natural order of things and makes me want to cry. **CS**


**SWEET:** Why make something savoury when you can make it sweet? Why? Why?

Only one thing in the world is improved by adding salt, and that's vinegar crisps. Sugar makes everything better, so why spurn it for something cows like to lick?

I once loved a man who preferred salt popcorn to sweet. We could usually only afford one carton, so his solution was to get a mix of both. It didn't work. So, I married someone who orders sweet, even though he prefers salt, and lets me eat most of it. When it comes to popcorn, if it's not sweet, then neither am I. **FM**

# Question 78

# Classic cars:
# Mini or Beetle?

**MINI:** My first car; my every car; the best car in the whole, wide world and my one, true motoring love.

When you drive a Mini, you're driving a Monte Carlo Rally winner. Every road is Brands Hatch, the world is a better place and the birds sing more sweetly, as you burn up even the fastest sports cars at the lights. Sure, they'll pass you almost immediately, but by then you've made your point. Acceleration, manoeuvrability, panache, cheek; it's the drive of your life and until you've driven a Mini, you've never really driven.

I loved my last Cooper so much, I had to sell it. I was obsessed. It's a long story, but basically, by the end, nobody could bounce a ball near my car and live. I'm still traumatised, but another of my old Minis lives on the Isle of Man and I visit often.

I could bore you with stories of how I've turned it on a tiddlywink and parked where only Smart cars dare to tread, but I won't. Suffice to say that, although the Beetle is the people's car, the Mini is the driver's car; and even if the Beetle can claim to be the world's best-selling car, everyone knows the Mini is by far the best loved. **FM**


**BEETLE:** One of my girlfriends had a Mini Cooper and I have to agree that they are lovely cars – to look at. In order to sit in it, I had to pull my knees virtually up to my ears and rest my buttocks on the glove compartment.

I also concede that it could well be a lovely car to drive – that is, until you hit something hard, like a cyclist or an air-pocket, and then the next thing you see will be a fireman gently trying to remove the grille from your head. The original VW Beetle, on the other hand, was roomier, safer, and a lot more robust. And it was designed by Porsche. Although initially driven mainly by the Nazi hierarchy, this car was so good that the first bulk order for the Beetle was placed in 1945 – by the British Army. **WOL**

# Question 79

# Water: fizzy or still?

**FIZZY:** I think it's outrageous, decadent and bourgeois that you are expected to pay for water just because someone put it in a bottle, but at least with the fizzy water there's been some sort of aerating process involved. I like to think that the water is free, but I'm paying for the bubbles. **WOL**


**STILL:** If you really want to pay for something, buy a packet of Alka Seltzer and pop it in your glass, because that's precisely what the fizzy stuff tastes of. Still water may not be particularly interesting, but at least it doesn't mimic a hangover cure. The only mildly palatable thing about fizzy is its ability to reverse the laws of physics. Only when dealing with gas-filled water can you guarantee that what goes down must come up. Eventually. **FM**

# Question 80

# Carrot or stick?

**CARROT:** I respond much better to being bribed than beaten. Cajole me, encourage me, offer me cake and I'll be putty in your hands. Promise me some dark chocolate, or some Arctic Roll, and I'll climb Everest, if required. But shout at me, or threaten me, and I'll either cry, or dig my heels in. Either way, it won't bring out the best in me. I simply can't be doing with the nasty, non-carrot way of doing things. The stick is for fascist regimes and Fat Club, it's not for civilised society and it's certainly not for me. **CS**


**STICK:** Both the carrot and the stick are methods for getting a human, or an animal, to do something that it wouldn't do otherwise. The governing classes realised long ago that these beasts of burden worked better if they were offered carrots rather than a beating, and the labouring animals also felt that this was preferable.

But the carrot is an insidious tool of manipulation, blinding you, the worker, to the fact that you are still shackled and still undervalued. You are still being asked to do something you'd rather not do and, if you're doing it for a carrot (which, by the way, is being dangled from a stick), you can bet that what you are doing is worth at least two carrots, if not a whole bag. But who gets that? The governing classes, of course.

Only when you beasts of burden realise that carrots are no substitute for freedom, will you rise above your dreary, repetitive, mechanistic lives and overthrow the carrot-wielding scum. But be careful not to attack innocent vegetarians in the process. **WOL**

# Question 81

# Cinderella or Snow White?

**CINDERELLA:** Snow White has no social life. She's stuck in a forest, cooking and cleaning for six elderly miners and one youngster with special needs. Where's the fun in that? No, the character to be in *Snow White* is definitely the Wicked Queen.

Cinders had problems with her step-mother too, but at least she got out and strutted her stuff at the ball. In some versions of the story, she goes out three nights in a row and wears a different dress every night. Wow. A personal counsellor with magic powers; free transport; great clothes; and a rich, handsome bloke looking high and low for you, while you quietly bide your time in order to humiliate people who have been mean to you. This story is the ultimate girl-bliss.

Nor should we forget that Cinderella had actually spent some quality time with her prince before she married him. It wasn't a case of "I dislodged that apple from your throat – you're mine, babe". And nobody was trying to kill her, either. **FM**


**SNOW WHITE:** I feel Snow White has a far, far better time. She gets to come back from the dead for starters - *douze points* there, surely? She also has the consistently superior wardrobe. Cinders has to dress in rags, until she gets to go to a couple of dances. But even then, any ground she makes up on the garment front is completely lost due to those fearsome glass slippers. One false move in those babies and her feet are ticker tape.

It's the same story in the man department. Snow White is clearly better off. Whilst waiting for Prince Right, she got the full attention of seven small men with time on their hands and, when her prince arrived, he was considerate enough not to have a deep-seated foot fetish. **CS**

# Question 82

# Crosswords:
# quick or cryptic?

**QUICK:** If I do the quick crossword, I have an outside chance of:
- a)   Understanding the clues.
- b)   Finishing it.
- c)   Not looking like a sad person trying to impress.
- d)   Not taking after my father.
- e)   Not making myself feel stupid.
- f)   Not setting the paper on fire, due to lack of a) and b). **CS**


**CRYPTIC:** On the train, or in an airport departure lounge, having a go at a cryptic crossword sends out a particular signal to other passengers. It tells them you are intelligent and confident, and this makes you attractive to women. Men will admire you, too, because they will assume you are a spy. Everyone knows that MI6 communicates with its agents through cryptic crossword clues. This makes you even more attractive to women.

If you ever manage to complete a cryptic crossword, you should always take it along to job interviews, because it is widely acknowledged to be the equivalent of 137 grade A passes at A-level. **WOL**

# Question 83

# Olympics:
# Summer or Winter?

**SUMMER:** I can watch the Australian rowing team wandering about in the world's tightest Lycra, I can laugh at the synchronised diving, the solo synchronised swimming and the speed walkers. The Brits have an outside chance of winning a medal, I can dust down and air my anti-marathon rant (it's not a sport, it's a form of torture) and best of all, the female shot putters make me feel that perhaps I don't need plastic surgery after all. **CS**


**WINTER:** The way in which the Olympics have evolved tells you a lot about modern civilisation. The Games have become a crass, overblown circus, where the criteria for what counts as an Olympic sport would be unrecognisable to the ancient Greeks and to Pierre de Coubertin, who re-introduced the Games in 1896.

Given my general lack of enthusiasm for them, I tend to prefer the quieter, more sedate affair that is the Winter Olympics. I like the fact that there isn't so much fuss about them, that they don't seem to go on and on for months, and they aren't traditionally dominated by the United States. Perhaps it's precisely because the Americans don't 'win' the Winter Olympics, and often finish behind Norway, that there's less made of them.

The Summer Olympics are essentially a Harvey Wallbanger, with cocktail brollies and a sparkler, whereas the Winter Olympics are a glass of apple schnapps, drunk warm by the fireplace, on a bearskin rug. **WOL**

# Question 84

# Mozart or Beethoven?

**MOZART:** I don't know much about classical music, but I know what I like and I like Mozart. The man was responsible for some of the most beautiful sounds that will ever be heard by the human ear. The fact that his music combines passion with subtlety means I never feel bullied, or harangued, like I do when I listen to Beethoven. The German could never have written the Countess's aria from *The Marriage of Figaro* – at least, not with the same quiet intensity of feeling. I'm sure he'd have felt the need for a rousing chorus, or some breast beating, and the whole thing would have been ruined.

It has been suggested that listening to Mozart makes one more intelligent, something that just ices the cake as far as I'm concerned. Beethoven is far too much and far too deaf. **CS**


**BEETHOVEN:** Ludwig beats Wolfgang for four reasons.

1) Tunes: Beethoven has the higher hummability rating. I can hum Beethoven any time, anywhere. Mozart has more notes and fewer good tunes. Try humming *O, Isis and Osiris* from *The Magic Flute* – it's not much fun, is it? Now try the *Ode to Joy*. There, that's why Ludwig is King of the Ringtones.

2) Hero-worship: Mozart never wrote a symphony for Napoleon. Not his fault - he was dead - but still a glaring omission from any composer's canon. True, Beethoven regretted dedicating the *Eroica* to Bonaparte, but oops, too late to take it back! Great tune for a great man. Top marks.

3) Economy: Da-da-da-dummm! Immortality in four notes. The most famous four notes in music.

4) *Fortissimo*, please: Beethoven wrote better music when he was deaf than Mozart did with a fully functional set of eardrums. **FM**

# Question 85

# Brown sauce or ketchup?

**BROWN SAUCE:** In 1524, Henry VIII announced a competition to find something the English could use to liven up their dull and tasteless food. After twenty years of searching, some Spaniards returned from the lower Andes with a 'plump fruit' known to the Aztecs as 'tomati'. Once the new fruit reached the British Isles, it was quickly turned into a gooey pulp to splodge onto our fish and chips. "That'll do us" we said and for almost 350 years we would countenance no other sauce. But at the end of the nineteenth century, due to a misplaced decimal point, an excessive amount of dates, molasses, tamarind extract and spices arrived at Southampton docks from the various corners of the British Empire. In order to alleviate the problem, Parliament rushed through the New Sauce (Emergency) Act 1899, which stipulated that these ingredients must be mixed with tomato ketchup until they were all used up. Ever since then, these sauces have become symbols for two very different socio-political viewpoints, with traditionalists, conservatives and royalists championing ketchup and progressive, pro-diversity, pro-parliamentarians supporting brown sauce. I am with the Brown Sauce Party. **WOL**


**KETCHUP:** This Question asks us to choose between the sacred and the profane. Ketchup has moral right on its side. Brown sauce comes from the dark side; it is the juice squeezed from the udders of Satan's cow. I cannot, I really cannot, understand why anyone puts that evil stuff on their food. Ketchup enhances what you eat; it makes fish fingers taste like ambrosia and chips like nectar. Brown sauce is…well, it's very brown, contains dark, unidentifiable flecks, and makes me very depressed. There's not a single meal out there that deserves to be inflicted with brown sauce. **CS**

# Question 86

# C. S. Lewis or Tolkien?

**C.S. LEWIS:** Let me define my terms, here. When I say C.S. Lewis, I actually mean the *Narnia* books. I've not read anything else by the man and I don't intend to. I was ten and I had no idea that these wonderful stories had strong Christian overtones. I was oblivious to all that and spent a very happy summer reading them all. The first and, for my money, far and away the best book, *The Lion, the Witch and the Wardrobe*, had me gasping for breath. The idea of a secret world inside a cupboard just blew me away. The evil queen, the land forever frozen in the clutches of winter, and the brave Aslan, all had me hooked and I couldn't stop until I'd found out what happened to the country and those that fought for it. The books had such scope and imagination, it was autumn before I left my chair.

I've never seen the point of hobbits and you can't go near anything by J.R.R. Tolkien without encountering a surfeit of the damn things, so I couldn't possibly choose him. **CS**


**TOLKIEN:** No God; fewer talking animals; far fewer kids.

I can forgive J.R.R. anything — even Tom Bombadil's singing — for the unsurpassed enchantment of *The Hobbit* alone. But *Smith of Wootton Major* made me feel like I'd swallowed a star. **FM**

# Question 87

# At the cinema: trailers or credits?

**TRAILERS:** Credits are boring, boring, boring. I don't care who did what. If the man who gripped the dolly really wanted his contribution acknowledged, he should have enrolled in a drama school and not one that specialised in gripping dollies. Then his name would have been seen at the beginning of the film - and by me. However, I do want to know what films are scheduled to be released, and I enjoy deciding whether I might like to go and see them. It's all part of the anticipation of the film to come; it's the foreplay leading to the actual consummation. Once the deed's over, it's time for a fag and off we go home. **CS**


**CREDITS:** Sit back down, or at least get out of my eyeline quickly, damn you. Just because the credits are rolling doesn't mean the film is over, you know. I want to see the *whole* film, do you understand? All the way through to the end. By which time you may well be on a bus home and you'll find out later that you missed some brilliant out-takes, or some other special little gift they tacked on the end to reward the patience of thoughtful people like me.

I can live with missing the forthcoming attractions, but once the film has started, I'm with it all the way. It's not only interesting to check out the locations, or to see what that song was they played, it's important to show respect to the people that made the film. The best boy, key grip, lighting cameraman, et al, slaved for months, maybe even years, so you could enjoy the film. So now you're here, have the grace to sit still, keep your big mouth shut and learn something until the lights go up. **FM**

# Question 88

# Gin or vodka?

**GIN:** Gin (and tonic) is an afternoon 'cooler' in a plush Singaporean hotel; or a pre-dinner drink in Rome's Piazza Navona, watching the Italian girls swish by in their summer dresses.

Vodka is a nightmarish trudge through the streets of Faliraki, stepping over the copulating teenagers and piles of sick; or it's trying to get through Taunton on a Friday night without being glassed, or kicked to death.

Maybe I'm showing my age a bit here, but I would go for gin. **WOL**


**VODKA:** It's so sleighs, it's so big fur hat, it's so *Dr Zhivago*. Sipping a vodka and tonic makes you feel as though you have snow beneath your feet and revolution in your heart. Gin is mother's ruin; it tastes foul and makes me sick as dog. **CS**

# Question 89

# Jumper or shirt?

**JUMPER:** Jumpers figure largely in my Norwegian submarine captain fantasies, but that's not the only reason I like to see a man wearing something I can snuggle up to.

Unless it's a very hot day, I find a man who deliberately chooses a shirt very disconcerting. What's he thinking? He's wearing something that is almost what he wears to work. He's only a tie away from formality. Why is he doing this? Is he still on duty? Can he ever relax? I can't. I'm forever waiting for him to say "Must pop back to the office – the ink-jet cartridges were playing up something terrible".

Anyway, why would a man wear a shirt to work when he can wear a polo-neck with a jacket and look like Illya Kuryakin?

A man in a jumper is altogether more attractive, more hunky and oozes reliability. He's an individual who doesn't take life too seriously. You know he feels good, you know school's out and he's unequivocally all yours. **FM**


**SHIRT:** Just imagine the scene: the early morning light is breaking in through your window, you turn over to place a loving arm across Ashley Judd, but she's not there. You throw back the sheets, pull on your boxers, and go to see where she's got to. You enter the kitchen and there she is, drinking a glass of orange juice. She smiles at you, cheekily. She is wearing your shirt, with just a few buttons fastened - and nothing else! Jeez, you saucy minx - get straight back to bed. Now!

Imagine the scene again, but this time she's wearing your chunky, cable-knit, polo-neck jumper. It just doesn't work. Well, not so well. **WOL**

# Question 90

# Harry Potter or
His Dark Materials?

**HARRY POTTER:** A friend of mine cried his eyes out on the tube, in front of hundreds of commuters, because he'd just read the end of *The Amber Spyglass*. I was the one who told him to read the *Dark Materials* trilogy, so when he confessed his emotional response, he expected me to understand. Yet all I could think was, damn, did I miss something there?
Philip Pullman is a fantastic writer and the worlds he creates are much more complex, subtle and exotic than J. K. Rowling's, but although he takes me for a wild ride, he leaves my heart behind. Deep within all the Blytonesque adventurousness of the Potter books is a kernel of real humanity, of love, that makes me blub like a baby as soon as anybody falls off their broom. **FM**


**HIS DARK MATERIALS:** There really isn't enough room here to explain how magnificent these books are. They have challenged me; they have transported me to parallel universes; they have even changed the way I think. Following Lyra through her physical, emotional and metaphysical journey has been one of the most fantastic literary experiences I've ever had. There was never a single moment when I could predict where the story would go, or when I lost interest in any of the characters. Pullman manages to entwine ideas about life, death, sexuality, religion and duty into a rollicking good story. His invention of the daemon (the outward manifestation of a person's soul) alone should be enough to ensure literary immortality and the world's admiration. I cannot tell you how many times I went past my train stop because I was reading these; they made me lose all sense of my own time and space.
Harry who? **CS**

# Question 91

# Ghost or UFO?

**GHOST:** I saw a ghost once. It appeared at just the right time to save me from making a move on a beautiful foreign girl. At the time I wasn't too appreciative, but a few years later, I heard that the same girl had stabbed a man because he refused to commit to a relationship after having slept with her. Good ghost.

My brother has also seen a ghost. At first she seemed to be quite harmless; a little Victorian girl who wandered about the house, oblivious to what was happening around her. Then one night, he woke up to see the ghost-child standing right through the middle of his bed, looking him straight in the eye, waving her arms around and laughing malevolently. Bad ghost.

The point of these (true) stories is to show that there are a surprising number of very ordinary, normal, sensible people who have had a brush with the spirit world. But the majority of people who claim to have had UFO experiences seem to be dumb Americans. Another thing to consider is that, although my brother's ghost experience was evidently traumatic, at least he wasn't rogered up the backside with a metal probe – at least, not by the ghost. **WOL**


**UFO:** OK, I've never seen either, but despite the unpleasant possibility of being probed, sighting a UFO is definitely the top score of weirdness.

Everybody will know the truth about ghosts eventually. You just have to die to find out. However, proving the existence of UFOs would create *bona fide* history and mean guaranteed immortality for the first person to do it.

UFO beats ghost because people have been seeing ghosts forever, to no apparent avail. But produce a little green man and you've established conclusively that we're not alone in the universe. A ghost is essentially just another person – but dead. A UFO brings a new species, new hope, a whole raft of possibilities. The world will be changed and humanity's whole outlook transformed forever.

Put that up against the usual calibre of messages from beyond the grave ("Auntie Enid says take the doilies out of the cupboard – there's moths in there") and the dream of inter-galactic entente suddenly seems even more diverting. **FM**

# Question 92

# Ella Fitzgerald or Billie Holliday?

**ELLA:** She was the First Lady of Song, wasn't she? If I'm going to listen to anything vaguely jazzy - and it's not something I make a habit of - it's got to be Ella. I can relax, because I know she's going to do it just like I dream it should be done. Lulling, smooth, rich; nothing ever jars with Ella.
Billie sounds like a female Satchmo. She's just too idiosyncratic. You never know what's coming next and that's no good, especially when the purpose of jazz is to send people to sleep. And *God Bless The Child* - what's that about? No, really, I haven't the slightest idea. What *is* it about? **FM**


**BILLIE:** Ella might have had the technical edge - her voice is beautiful and has enormous range - but it's cold. Whatever she sings sounds the same. It might be a cliché, but it's also a fact that Billie sang from the very bowels of her being and that makes her my choice. In her last album, *Lady in Satin*, there is a world of experience. Her voice has become slight and seems more vulnerable, but in it you can hear all the cigarettes she ever smoked, all the love affairs that went so very wrong, and all the dirty jokes she ever told. It's as revealing as reading her diary. I want a song to tell a story and Billie was the greatest storyteller ever. **CS**

# Question 93

# Ben and Jerry's or
Häagen-Dazs?

**BEN AND JERRY'S:** Ice cream is childhood's favourite, fun treat. But when people get older, they worry that eating ice cream in public will make them look stupid and juvenile. They fear they won't be taken seriously – unless, that is, they are seen to be paying through the nose for a more sophisticated version, with aspirational, bourgeois, faux-European branding.
Ben and Jerry have a very different philosophy. Going up to the counter and asking for "Two tubs of Chubby Hubby and a Chunky Monkey, please" is a real test of humility. It says, "I have come to know myself and have accepted the infinitesimally small speck of nothingness that my existence represents in the scheme of things. Aware that my life is brief and inconsequential, I do not care one jot what other people think if they see me eating something which contains fudge-covered, peanut butter-filled pretzels". Mind you, you still have to pay through the nose for it. **WOL**


**HÄAGEN-DAZS:** All ice cream is good and Chubby Hubby is better than most. I'm also very happy to wish all power to Ben and Jerry's corporate ethos, but the crux of the matter is that I need real chocolate. Preferably Belgian. All the time. "Chocolatey" pieces simply won't do. Is it real chocolate, or is it "chocolatey"? The question of chocolate veracity is important, because in my world, even Hershey's doesn't count. Call me a purist, but until Ben and Jerry can guarantee me that they use nothing but real, 100 per cent, unadulterated, EU approved chocolate, I cannot completely forsake Häagen-Dazs. **FM**

# Question 94

# Escalator: stand or walk?

**STAND:** I often have to be at work before eight in the morning, so if I want to reach the top of the escalator alive, I stand and let it take me. I don't walk up it. I have discovered that standing has many underrated advantages.  If I'm especially tired, it gives me the opportunity to rest my head on the person standing in front of me; it gives me a few extra seconds of peaceful contemplation before tackling the outside world again, and I can stare at the people travelling in the other direction. Walking is for those who want calf muscles like a springbok. **CS**


**WALK:** Oh good grief, get out of my way, will you? Are you really so lazy that you can't be bothered to move, just because the stairs are moving for you? Let me explain - the idea is that you use them as you would normal stairs, but lo, you get where you're going *quicker*.
Come on, step aside. If you're suddenly going to come to a dead halt, because you're so amazed to be riding on the incredible, enchanted staircase, please have the decency to stand on the right, so I can get past your inert bulk and on with my life. **FM**

# Question 95

# Museum or gallery?

**MUSEUM:** There's more variety in a museum. In a gallery, all you get are pictures and sculptures – and you can look at pictures in books.

In a museum, you get all sorts of different things, such as: bits of Charles I's bloodstained shirt; life-size plaster casts of Trajan's column; actual Lancaster bombers; various, assorted dead bodies; stuffed giant elk; whole steam locomotives; fossilised Viking poo; Franz Ferdinand's bullet-ridden car; the spear that killed Captain Cook; Marshal Davout's baton; and more dinosaurs than you can shake a thousand-year-old Mesopotamian battery at. Like I said, a tad more diversity.

Galleries have their place, but on the whole, give me artefacts, not arty-farty. **FM**


**GALLERY:** Paintings, photographs, installations, sculptures…I can't get enough of them. Every artist presents us with a whole new world, a whole different perspective and a wholly unique experience.

By contrast, museums often disappoint me. They always seem to be dark, they insist on displaying hundreds and hundreds of what is essentially the same thing (one Roman coin looks pretty much like another) and everything is shrivelled beyond recognition. If I wanted to look at old gardening implements, dead animals, or a dirty shirt, then I'd visit my father's garden shed. **CS**

# Question 96

# Motorbike or sports car?

**MOTORBIKE:** Passes the 'cool' test hands down.

Motorbike: Steve McQueen (*The Great Escape*); Dennis Hopper (*Easy Rider*); Marlon Brando (*The Wild One*); Che Guevara (*The Motorcycle Diaries*).

Sports Car: Idiots; tosspots; sexual inadequates; Jeremy Clarkson. **WOL**


**SPORTS CAR:** There is a common assumption that women in offices fancy hunky motorcycle couriers. This is an urban myth, as any female who has taken a delivery from a rancid, sweat-soaked biker boy will tell you. The lad may look all leathered-up and hot to trot, but you'd faint from the stink long before he'd got his helmet off.

Motorbikes are for people who don't want, or need, a significant other. They signal commitment-phobia like a lighthouse. It's the difference between Steve McQueen in *The Great Escape* and Steve McQueen in *Bullitt*. The biker prefers to travel alone, but if he must take a passenger along for the ride, she has to play the Woman in the Iron Mask.

I don't mind if the object of my affection needs a big, red, shiny, 660 bhp penis extension, just so long as I get the luxury of a proper seat to myself and someone who cares that I did my hair before I came out. **FM**

# Question 97

# Schrödinger's Cat or Pavlov's Dogs?

**SCHRÖDINGER'S CAT:** Theoretically, take one box. Put in a radioactive nucleus and a canister of poison gas. Add one theoretical cat. Close the box and lock it. If the nucleus decays, it emits a particle that triggers an apparatus which opens the canister and kills the cat. Brilliant! I only have two problems with this. The first is: why must this experiment be theoretical? The second is that, despite the fact that the cat isn't real, I still feel this was a wasted opportunity and Schrödinger should have imagined a box big enough to house many cats, preferably not theoretical.
But overall, killing make-believe cats is preferable to taunting real dogs. **CS**


**PAVLOV'S DOGS:** Pavlov would ring a bell before feeding his dogs. "Yummy! Dinnertime!" the dogs would think, and start salivating. Pavlov noted that the dogs would begin salivating when the bell rang, before he even put the food out. This was because the dogs had learned to associate bells with feeding time. The next thing he did was to ring the bell and not give them food. They still salivated. What did this prove? Thanks to Pavlov, it is now an indisputable scientific fact that dogs are stupid.
You can try this experiment at home. If you don't have a dog, try it on your husband, or a child. Now, try it on a cat.  It won't work. Why? Because cats are smart. **WOL**

# Question 98

# Cooking or gardening?

**COOKING:** I hate being outside. I hate digging. I can kill a plant without touching it. I hate insects. I hate slimy, soily things and I can't stand the fact that, if you've been gardening, the only way to get your nails clean is to wash your hair.

Cooking is therapeutic, it's calming, it has machines to do the difficult bits, you can drink while you're doing it and you can eat the results of your labour straight away. **CS**


**GARDENING:** Western civilisation has long taken the words of Genesis 1:28 - that Man should subdue the earth and have dominion over it - as a license to exploit and despoil nature. So we have deforested, polluted, exterminated and laid waste the natural environment from whence we came and upon which we depend.

Gardening is a way of exercising our dominion, but with minimal impact. It's a kind of 'sustainable dominion' where we can wield our power over the natural world in a restrained and controlled way, gently working with nature to achieve beauty and bounty. It is an attempt to reclaim the Garden of Eden that we first lost through the misuse of our power.

Alternatively, gardening could simply be about sitting in the shed, listening to a football match and flicking through an old porn mag – also known as "Just doing some potting". **WOL**

# Question 99

# Microscope or telescope?

**MICROSCOPE:** When I was about seven years old, my two best birthday presents were a chemistry set and a microscope. After a month of experimenting with my chemistry set, I had only discovered one important fact: when mixed together, any four chemicals – any at all – will always make 'brown'.

There obviously wasn't a great deal of fun to be had with chemistry, so I concentrated on my microscope and the study of lycanthropy – or, to be more precise, monitoring my little brother to see if he was turning into a werewolf. Despite overwhelming evidence that he was, I never did find wolf cells in his blood, but I had fun persuading him to let me cut his finger every time there was a full moon. **WOL**


**TELESCOPE:** Thank you for that, Dr Frankenstein.

The bottom line is that microscopes are for arrogant introverts and telescopes are for self-effacing extroverts. I don't want to spend all day looking at tiny bugs; I want to see the epic grandeur of the universe. Look through a microscope and you see small stuff that makes you feel big. Look though a telescope and you see big stuff that makes you feel small. Microscopes make small things look big, but telescopes make big things that look small (because they are far away) look big again. Telescopes give us a much healthier perspective on our existence.

Telescopes show us the biggest possible picture, but microscopes can be useful for indicating whether or not Raquel Welch just popped out of your tear duct. **FM**

# Question 100

# Fame or fortune?

**FAME:** Never mind the money, give me immortality. It's all about the legend you leave behind. People will be talking about Ghandi forever, but he didn't have a single sponsorship deal. As long as we're talking fame and not infamy – and we are – I'd die happy if I knew I'd be in the history books and inspiring generations to come with my all-round fabness. Choosing fortune over fame is basically announcing that you don't care about being remembered for bringing peace to the world, or single-handedly averting a Martian invasion, so long as after you're dead, your kids can afford to fly first-class. **FM**


**FORTUNE:** My ideal situation combines affluence and anonymity. Anybody with the combination of wealth and fame risks becoming a target for all sorts of scoundrels and ne'er-do-wells. But if I had a fortune and nobody knew me, it would be possible for me enjoy my wealth in peace and quiet. I could also give the occasional large donation to needy orphans, or an orang-utan sanctuary. You could help me do this by recommending this book to your friends and family, or by purchasing multiple copies. I get less than 20p for every book sold, so save some orang-utans and buy lots. **WOL**

# Question 101

# Marmite or death?

**MARMITE:** To love Marmite is to belong to a select club. There's an immediate connection when you meet a fellow Marmiter, just as fellow Mini drivers, or fellow pipe smokers, give each other a knowing nod when their paths cross. We are so comfortable in our love for Marmite that we don't mind when someone declares their hatred for it. We accept that position, partly out of self-interest ("More for me then!"), but also because Marmiters are more reasonable people than anti-Marmiters.

Marmiters are quiet, unassuming types, who like to spread reconstituted brewer's yeast on their toast. There's nothing sinister about it. We don't brag, force you to witness it, or demand special rights because of it. We have nothing against non-Marmiters, but non-Marmitism is just the beginning of the slippery slope towards anti-Marmitism. If you don't like Marmite - fine. But if you rail against people who do like it, you object to its very existence and you would willingly renounce life because of it - well, go on then. Choose death - all of you. Then the world will belong to us. **WOL**


**DEATH:** Death. Every time. Take me away from a world that contains this vile pus of Beelzebub's bubos. That is, unless the Grim Reaper smells of yeast extract, and I bet he does. But what if Marmite *is* death, lurking in a small, deceptively unassuming, brown pot? Every time I come within smelling distance of the stuff, I fear for my existence. I'd rather kiss a rabid dog than someone who'd just eaten Marmite. I'm convinced that death by Marmite can be incurred just by accidental inhalation and frankly, I can't think of a worse way to go.

Think about it — it's made of yeast. You know, the stuff that gives you thrush? One day you're douching with yoghurt to get rid of something; the next, you're spreading extract of it on to a baguette. Why would you deliberately put something in your body that you would otherwise go to a doctor to exorcise? It's evil; it's wrong. It's the devil's bile. On toast. **FM**

If you've enjoyed The Classic Questions and fancy joining
in the discussion, visit

# www.thequestions.co.uk

# Question 102

# The Questions books:
# Retro or Classic?

**RETRO:** Thanks to the Retro Questions, the fine art of Questioning is imbued with the added bonus of comforting nostalgia. If anything, they're actually a quicker way of finding a like mind than the Classic Questions, because the impassioned feelings of one's youth never fail to run fast and deep.

Even though it's always good to have a bitch with a fellow Escalator Walker about the dumbos who stand, there's something even more potent about finally finding someone who, like you, totally comprehends the socio-cultural impact of the Lolly Gobble Choc Bomb. The bond is far more profound. Your generation is calling you home.

The Retro Questions are the whole Question experience – and then some. **FM**


**CLASSIC:** The Classic Questions are the most important Questions. They are timeless, deal with strongly held beliefs, and are therefore the true litmus tests of the soul.

When you were young, you were influenced by fashion and hormones. Knowing whether a person prefers Dandelion and Burdock to Vimto, or Hector's House to Andy Pandy, doesn't let you understand their heartfelt desires in the same way as asking whether they want to share your bath or shower. Used wisely, these Classic babies will give you more insight into a person's soul than sitting for thousands of years on top of a mountain ever could. **CS**

*Fiona McCade: Having destroyed her good twin in the womb, Fiona is an only child. She spent her formative years trying to turn her parents' garage into the National Theatre of Yorkshire, so nobody was surprised when she went on to be a professional actress. This led to some theatre work, occasional film and TV parts and a great deal of temping.*

*While playing Emma Peel she got a nasty case of leather-burn, so she became a freelance writer, broadcaster and columnist for The Scotsman. She currently lives in Edinburgh with a tame Manxman and a large collection of Napoleonic literature.*

*Sticks make her aggressive, but carrots calm her down.*


*William O' Leary was raised in Yorkshire and the Isle of Man. Before university he travelled to North America where, in 1984, he helped Courtney Cox onto the stage during the filming of Bruce Springsteen's* Dancing in the Dark *video. Following higher education, he worked for the Carpathian Forestry Board before settling in New Zealand for five years where he found employment as a fireman, carpenter and artist's model. Returning to the UK to establish a moorhen sanctuary in Cumbria, William continues to eke out a living from fees received for his appearance in a series of Australian toilet roll commercials.*

*He has a very strong aversion to hobbits.*


*Cath Sutton: Cath was born in Surrey and is the middle sister of three, although she's never longed to visit Moscow. However, before and during studying at Manchester University she did travel to New Zealand, India and throughout Europe. Despite being a pogo stick prodigy and exhibiting a startling aptitude for this highly-skilled discipline throughout her childhood, she decided not to pursue it as a career and became a counsellor for a women's health organisation instead.*

*She's still waiting for someone to convince her that* Star Trek *(whatever the generation) isn't a cosmic waste of everyone's time and an unnecessary drain on the world's resources.*

Printed in the United Kingdom
by Lightning Source UK Ltd.
102623UKS00002B/123